AUG 1 7 2017

THE HOLISTIC DOG

Also by Laura Benko

The Holistic Home

THE HOLISTIC DOG

INSIDE THE CANINE MIND, BODY, SPIRIT, SPACE

STORIES BY LAURA BENKO

PHOTOGRAPHS BY SUSAN FISHER PLOTNER

Helios press

This book is dedicated to my favorite three: my husband, Johnny; my daughter, Luchia; and my dog, Yogi. You guys are my world. Love, Laura

For Judah, Sam, and Jordan, and Rosie—my rock 'n' roll. Always and forever, SFP

Contents

Acknowledgments   IX

Introduction   XI

The Inspiration: Our Dogs' Stories   XV

SECTION I   1

Space: Inside the Homes and Lives of Holistic Dogs   1

SECTION II   147

Mind: Inside the Canine Mind and Behavior, The Expert Interviews   147

Body: Inside the Canine Wellness and Health, The Expert Interviews   177

Spirit: Inside the Canine Soul, Psyche, and Beyond, The Expert Interviews   239

About the Author   268

Interview with the Author   269

About the Photographer   273

Interview with the Photographer   274

Index   278

Acknowledgments

First, I'd like to thank all the incredible canines featured in this book. You are all extraordinary, sentient little souls that deeply touch all those who know you, and now, my heart too. It's been a privilege to get to know you better through your adoring parents—whom I'm also greatly indebted to. Much gratitude to the Mind experts, Dr. Megan Maxwell, Annie Grossman, Evan Maclean, and Nina Ottosson. Thank you to the Body team: Clare Kearny, Randy Klein, Kim Freeman, Dr. Gene Giggleman, Laura Turley, Dr. Jill Elliot, and Dr. Gerald Post. To my Spirit squad, I'm deeply appreciative to Sarah Hauser, Kim Russo, Eileen Garfinkel, and Wendy Van de Poll. To Dr. Marty Goldstein, thank you for so tirelessly persevering for over thirty years in integrated veterinarian care, setting the groundwork for all that has unfolded in this field, and for your contribution to this book.

Nicole Frail, you are the most professional, reliable, and proficient editor an author could ever have. Thank you for all your hard work and continued support. Susan Fisher Plotner, thank you for taking such beautiful photographs that bring the stories and interviews to life, and for working so diligently to make this book everything it has become. Lisa and Carlos Rodriguez, I am so grateful to you both, and to your cover girl Sunny, for your presence, love and support. Thank you to Leigh and Jim Gardner, Katherine and Mary Benko, and my rock and best friend, Andrea Sanders. Deep admiration and gratitude go to Phillip Tyler Alden for being the most inspiring dog owner I have ever met and a big influence throughout this book. A million thank you's to my right hand in all I do: Desirée Guédez. Your dedication, reliability, and expertise enable me to achieve and succeed in so many ways. To my Big Daddy, Gene S. Benko, your generous heart, love of animals, and your effusive spirit will always be with me. To my mom, Barbara Benko, your love makes it all possible. Lastly, thank you to my most beloved trio: my man, Johnny Ceriello, my joy and light, Luchia Ceriello, and my sweet boy Yogi, you three occupy my mind, body, spirit, space, and heart forever. —Laura

I am so grateful to Laura Benko, my open-hearted partner on this inspiring journey. I could not have asked for greater dedication to, and affection for, our aspiration. What a rollicking ride, Laura!

Many thanks to all who welcomed me into their homes and helped me whisper their beloved canines into momentary supermodels. What a joy to meet you. Dog-sized thanks to Aunt Betty, Alexis Blood, Sally Cohen and Rocky Atkins, Nancy Goldberg, Emily Kandel, Martha Rizzoli, and Perry Ryan who found many of our eager participants. This book came to life with your enthusiastic support.

I am indebted to Nikki, without whom I could not leave my beloved Rosie for photoshoots far and wide. Nikki, you are cherished.

Mom and Dad, thank you for everything I am! Pamela, eagle-eyed, thank you for leading me to Laura. Finally, my S&Js, you have my heart. Thank you for your wholehearted love and unbounded humor. ILYMTYK! —Susan

Introduction

In my previous book, *The Holistic Home: Feng Shui for Mind, Body, Spirit, Space*, I talk about making the connections between your Mind, Body, and Spirit within yourself and your own Space. I share my clients' stories—as well as my own journey—of transformation in self and space. For 78 million people in the United States, their space is one where a dog resides. Those dogs are what help make those houses into homes. In *The Holistic Dog: Inside The Canine Mind, Body, Spirit, Space*, I wanted to show how these creatures have become so holistically integrated into our homes and lives, by telling their stories and showcasing them in their spaces. In the interviews, I delve into the Mind, Body, and Spirit components of 108 dogs. **Mind** covers the personality, behaviors, habits, and intellect of the dogs. The **Body** aspects are physical characteristics—nutrition, exercise, breed, health care, and wellness. **Spirit** delves into the undeniable emotional connections, the unspoken bonds, and the karmic lessons these canines have imbued in our lives.

The book begins with **Space** with Susan Fisher Plotner's stunning photographs of each dog—usually taken in a favorite spot of their home—and includes their wide-ranging stories. Having a dog is life-changing. You might find yourself getting up early to walk them when you never were a morning person before. You might even change vacation plans just so you can bring them along or buy a bigger car to fit them in or rush home from somewhere fun just to be with them. Their companionship is imprinted on endless family memories, and their connection with their devoted humans and the lessons they teach us are profound. These lessons are as varied as the breeds and personalities featured here, but some common themes often include exercise, patience, companionship, perseverance, second chances, socializing, or unconditional love.

For every dog included, I wanted the focus to be on them. That is why humans are not pictured in the photographs and the stories only contain the names of the dogs—not the family members. (In referring to the humans associated with the dogs, you'll find fluid terms such as the mom, the dad, companion, loved one, dog owner, human family member, etc. While there are raging debates as to the titles of "pet parents" versus "dog owners," I chose varying labels for the purpose of range and diversity, not as a statement on parenting or property ownership.)

In the second half of the book, the canine expert section offers insights from top canine authorities in Mind, Body, and Spirit. From behaviorists and researchers who probe into the canine mind, to integrated veterinarians that cover head-to-tail health aspects, to an animal grief counselor who helps navigate the spiritual aftermath of losing a pet, all of these experts and more share valuable insights and tips. Hopefully, after reading this book, you'll see the term *holistic* not as an elitist, eye-rolling expression of overindulged canine lifestyles, but as a way to genuinely understand, interact, and care for your dog by looking at all the parts that make this species whole. By doing so, your time with them can be even more rewarding, healthier, and more meaningful.

Wishing you all the best for you and your dog in Mind, Body, Spirit, and Space,

Laura Benko

The Inspiration: Our Dogs' Stories

Yogi

Irish Terrier | 8 years old | Laura's Dog

Here is my little guy. My gentle soul (unless this terrier sees a menacing-looking dog—then he might viciously bark at him). I named him Yogi because his demeanor is very chilled out inside the house and he's always doing downward dog like a veteran yogini. His favorite place to sit is behind the couch on the window seat, as pictured here. He loves to watch the world go by. He protects the house quite well. At least once throughout the day, I'll hide somewhere in the house, call him, and see if he can find me. He usually discovers me quickly, but there have been moments when I've been hiding in a closet or crouched down in the shower for a good ten minutes, asking myself, "What am I doing??"

I've always felt that Yogi is psychic, and after my husband heard me say it enough times, he challenged me to prove it by "psychically telling him to do something he's not allowed to do." For the next three days, I focused on telepathically telling Yogi that he's allowed to go on the couch. This is something that he's not allowed to do and had never even tried. Well, one morning as we came upstairs, there he was, all curled up in a ball on the black couch. When my husband yelled at him, I reminded him that I had psychically told him to do this! "Well, psychically tell him not to!" he said. I have no doubt that most dogs can easily tap into this sense because they are innately accustomed to reading the energy of their surroundings as a primordial function of survival.

My boy is a tender fella who gets easily startled by fireworks, thunder, loud voices, the smoke detector, and the toaster. He was my inspiration for a line of pure, all-natural dog products sold via my business, The Holistic Home Company. The Calm Dog spray has really helped him rise above those occasional vulnerable and shaky moments, and the bug spray is invaluable when we spend active time outdoors in the warmer weather. He tests each product and is with me every day at work, which sometimes explains why I get distracted. When he curls up in his "baby deer" pose, tucking his front paws underneath him, I must stop what I'm doing and give him some love.

I end each night and start each day cuddling up to him wherever he is lying, and for several minutes, I pet him and whisper to him that he's "my good boy." He's not much of a cuddler, but while tolerating my smothering, he will respond with a robust, content sigh. This is my assurance that all is right in the world.

Rosie

Beagle | 12 years old | Susan's Dog

When members of the family independently filled out a "What Dog is Best for Your Family" survey, all four results were unanimous: a Beagle! Rosie joined the family when they were living in England and was renamed after the country's national flower. At birth, her breeder called her Impish—apparently an inclination to do slightly cheeky things was evident from the start. The family soon discovered that Beagles are single-minded and are led by their unrivaled hound nose. To justify the treats bestowed on Rosie for just looking at them adoringly with her soulful "love me" eyes, they taught her to do various "circus tricks," like rolling over or jumping up on stonewalls. Even though Rosie has been found on all fours in the middle of the Thanksgiving table eating the apple pie and once unzipped a visitor's suitcase to eat an entire box of chocolates, her family all agrees: "We delight in her nature—gentle, earnest, and wholehearted—sprinkled with a spoonful of mischief."

When the family relocated back to New York, their otherwise indomitable Beagle was completely bewildered. The shock of airplane travel, new surroundings, stressed humans, and Hurricane Sandy upset her otherwise unflappable, even-tempered soul. She cried for months—and so did her mom. "Rosie is the uncomplicated essence of our family. Her presence—softly padding from room to room, following us like a shadow, curling up to the warmth of her brothers—is, quite simply, necessary. She is the deeply adored heart of our pack," says her mom.

Perhaps the most heartwarming and endearing revelation from the photographer who has spent an inordinate amount of time getting to know more than one hundred dogs, capturing their hearts and personalities, is what has turned out to become one of the greatest themes of *The Holistic Dog* book—the unquestionable, everlasting, pure love between dogs and their humans. "Rosie has my heart . . . it just never occurred to me that I would be overcome by an absolute driving impatience to run home after every shoot to hug her and tell her that although I had been with another, I love her best of all!"

I

Space

INSIDE THE HOMES AND LIVES OF HOLISTIC DOGS

In exploring the canine mind, body, spirit, and space, we begin with space. This section presents the dogs in their favorite environments, showcasing their physical space, along with the stories that delve into how they occupy a meaningful space in our hearts and everyday lives. For nearly all the dog owners interviewed, having a dog means that the simple act of coming home is more celebratory and domestic routines of play and companionship fill the household. Our canine family members indeed change the energy of our space and "liven up the home, making it a more spirited environment," as the mom of Cooper the English Setter says.

Their unique quirks within their spaces are endearing, like when Dexter prefers to sit with his dad on the couch *behind* him—not next to him—how Moose only sits on the third and fourth staircase step, or how Kevin and Birdy only sit upright like humans, with elbows casually resting on armrests. Sometimes their home habits can be a bit naughty or insistent. Winnie chooses only socks to hide all over the house, Pesto throws her bowl when her meal is late, and Chanel will not get into bed unless the covers are pulled back for her!

The sign in Mulligan's home says, HOME IS WHERE THE DOG IS, and many dog owners agree. They are a part of the family, and it is why we attentively care for them, rush home to be with them, and, as Lucy and Turbo's parents reveal, "We will often stay home more and entertain, just so we don't have to leave them!" It doesn't matter if they are sometimes challenging us by misbehaving, entertaining us with their idiosyncrasies, or enhancing the vibe with their unconditional love. We love them dearly, and we accept it all. It is why in Davey, Ruby, Molly, Toro, and Norma's multidog home, there's a warmhearted resignation by their dad, "Yes. My house smells like dog and I love it."

Jock

Cockapoo | 11 years old

Jock lives in England, is known to be "cheeky," and will bark in an angry way when someone whom he considers part of his pack leaves the house. He's not fond of departures. He knows when the housekeeper is getting ready to leave for the day and will let her know that he's displeased. He went through a phase of not liking pugs, but he seems to be over that now.

Even though his streak of apricot-colored hair down his back is his marked physical characteristic, most people confuse him for a lamb at first glance. Personality-wise, he is known for bringing people together, and, according to his family, he converts non-dog lovers into loyal admirers and won't give up until he is reassured that he has won them over.

Jock receives acupuncture, a monthly massage, hydrotherapy sessions, and only eats organic. *(For more on canine wellness, go to the Body section on page 177.)* He is a well-cared-for dog, but perhaps the best gift that his family says he gives is also one that many dogs give their loved ones: the present. "He makes us focus on the here and now."

"Few of us ever live in the present. We are forever anticipating what is to come or remembering what has gone."

—Louis L'Amour

Artwork: *Pietrasanta C04.30*, acrylic on canvas, Caio Fonseca.

Izzy

Border Collie Mix | 7 years old

Izzy is a rescue dog from eastern Washington State. At the shelter, her eyes seemed to convey, "Get me out of here!" and a connection was made. Whether it's a cross-country road trip or a family vacation, she's well behaved and hardly without her household members, whom she adores so much. On the rare occasion she's without them, she might rebelliously move all their shoes around.

She knows that when running shoes come out, it's a walk. A grab for keys means it's a ride, and when she's shown her doggie towel, she knows she will be going swimming.

If a family member is sick, she will stick close and not demand much attention of herself. She can open the refrigerator door and will wait at every street corner before crossing, and she gives her family ecstatic greetings when they return home. Her loved ones sum her up in three words: soulful, athletic, and affectionate.

Aries

Siberian Huskie | 5 years old

Siberian Huskies were originally bred to work as sled dogs. Their double coat can keep them warm even in arctic temperatures plunging to –75°F degrees, which explains why Aries is such a fan of the cold winters in Vermont. She loves being active outside and enjoys burrowing and prancing in the snow. Often, she will suddenly stop and then pounce down hard when she detects a mole or mouse deep beneath the snowy surface.

Aries's bushy tail and striking bright blue eyes are her most prominent features. "Oh, she knows she is beautiful!" says her dad. "I saw a photo of a litter of huskies and was drawn to Aries. When I got there, she was the only one left." The two of them are inseparable, and Aries has even figured out a way to keep it that way. When the family is in bed, Aries will only go to her mom to convey that she needs to go outside. When Mom gets up to let her out, Aries jumps in the bed to cuddle next to Dad!

Aries and her dad have created the popular video series *Rail Trails of America*. One of the reasons their trekking series has become so popular is that each segment offers invaluable visual footage with helpful tips such as "This part of the trail is shared with a private driveway" or "Now the woodsy trail stops and goes through a paved parking lot and resumes across the highway." Artifacts, bridge crossings, access points, and parking areas are all pointed out for each trail.

YouTube.com/IMRFilms
Facebook.com/RailTrailsofAmerica

Atticus

Havanese | 8 years old

Atticus likes to watch television. His veterinarian says that only 10 percent of dogs cannot differentiate between two- and three-dimensional images. Atticus not only watches television, but also tries to interact with the animals on screen. In fact, he recognizes commercials in which dogs appear and anticipates their arrival! His jaunty walk comes to a complete halt when he nears the vet or the groomer's, and then he has to be carried away.

One time, while being groomed, the groomer reported that he kept saying, "I want Mamma." She captured it on video and, sure enough, he seems to be saying, "I want Mamma"!

Interesting Dog Facts

- Dogs can see color! Greens, blues, yellow, and grays.
- Some dogs can sense blood sugar levels, anticipate seizures, and detect certain cancers.
- Dogs don't wag their tails when they're alone.
- Dogs' eyes contain a special membrane that allows them to see well in the dark.
- Dogs only sweat through the pads of their feet.
- The average city dog lives three years longer than a country dog.
- The longer a dog's nose, the more effective their cooling system.
- Dogs live an average of fifteen years.
- Dogs are sensitive to the earth's magnetic fields and prefer to poop in alignment with it.
- Dogs can hear four times the distance of humans.
- A dog's nose print is just as unique as a fingerprint.
- All puppies are born deaf.

(L to R): Ivan, Isabel, Lyla, Diego.

Isabel
Chihuahua | 14 years old

Diego
Chihuahua | 13 years old

Lyla
Beagle/hound mix | 4 years old

Ivan
Chihuahua | 2 years old

Never a dull moment!" is how this four-dog household is described. That being said, order, discipline, exercise, and playtime are all integral parts of their daily regimen to avoid having what their caregivers call "misbehaved or bored pets." They go on to say, "We see too many dogs who spend half their lives in crates, who get relegated to the backyard once the children are tired of their new puppy, who are starved for affection, are never exercised, or who are treated like toys and encouraged to bark incessantly for attention because their owners think it's cute." None of these scenarios exist here.

Since they spend a great deal of time with their dogs individually as well as all together as a group, it has allowed them to discover each one's idiosyncrasies and preferences. There are basically two cliques within the pack: the old timers who sleep a lot during the day and the young ones who chase one another around the house and yard. Diego is the leader, doesn't like his front paws touched, and has to run into the living room to "kill" one of his stuffed animals before he will eat his dinner. If a toy is tossed that he's not interested in fetching, he will point to the one he wants to play with. Isabel was a rescue and doesn't like people outside the house. Lyla, the Beagle/Hound mix, has grown up knowing the Chihuahuas are in charge. She housetrained herself by watching the other dogs and loves to have her armpits scratched. Ivan is the only dog who chooses to get under the blankets and curl up next to his humans and will never challenge Diego. As a pack, they keep one another company and will even put themselves to bed if their parents are staying up too late. "They sense our moods, they keep us laughing, and they bring vitality to our home."

Pepper

Collie | 6 months old

Collies are known for their agility and intelligence, and those two qualities are exactly what Pepper's family finds to be most impressive about her. At only five months old, Pepper astounded her family with her intellect. To keep her busy, they got her an "interactive smart toy" in which she had to get the treats out from under several plastic cups that were covering them. If she was able to remove the cups and get the treats, she was supposed to then figure out how to turn the toy around to find more hidden treats that were also covered by plastic. They thought it would keep her busy for an hour. She figured the whole thing out in five minutes. Now she can do it in around five seconds. *(For more about dog games and puzzles, go to Mind: Nina Ottosson, Dog Toy and Puzzle Inventor Interview, on page 170.)*

Outside, she likes to kick it up a notch and jump through Hula-Hoops and weave in and out of the family's legs, but inside, she's a calming presence in a "crazy household" who likes to sit *on top* of her crate while the family is eating dinner. She's become friendly with the other pet of the house—Clementine the bunny—although that friendship is still new and is approached with caution.

"Happiness is a warm puppy." —Charles Schulz

Shane

German Shorthaired Pointer | 4 years old

Shane has show dog lineage in his blood. His grandfather was a show dog champion, and Shane has the same identical large patch on his haunch. Shane has an American Kennel Club championship, which then leads to the Westminster Kennel Club Dog Show. His parents say the AKC professionals love Shane's "perfect gait," and when he's "on point and identifying prey, his stance is classic." His parents go on to add, "Although many people comment on what a great-looking hunting dog he is or how handsome he is, we remind him that beauty is only skin deep and his character is what matters." Every day before 7 a.m., he joins his parents for an off-leash hike through a thousand-acre stretch of woodlands. Shane knows when his orange hunting vest comes out that he's going up to the woods. Out in nature is his favorite place to be—besides his bed in front of the fireplace. When he's outside, his family calls him The Poet because he sits and gazes at the trees and reflectively observes his surroundings. He can be pitiless to a pesky squirrel, yet intuitively protective to a child when needed. His family says, "He's a breath of fresh air—always full of energy, a winning mischievous smile, and an energetic tail wagging anywhere, anytime in the house."

Ace

Pug | 9 years old

"Ace melts our hearts with affection! He thinks he's a lap dog and will climb onto a lap even if there is no room for him. He follows me everywhere—even waiting outside the shower," his companion said. Ace likes to spend most of his day chasing airplanes in the yard.

- Pugs are the largest dog in the Toy group.
- They are easily susceptible to colds since their noses are so short.
- A group of pugs is called a grumble.

Cookie Nutella

Chocolate Labrador | 13 years old

Cookie has a deep love for challah (Jewish braided bread) and tennis balls. Unfortunately, she chews and eats the tennis balls and has had to endure a few operations to remove them. Her family says she loves people, and, when out for a walk, she will always approach the dog owners first before the dogs themselves. She loyally guards the house when no one is home and will only fall into a deep sleep, snoring loudly, when her family is home and conversing.

Penny

F2 Miniature Goldendoodle | 6 years old

Penny's divine connection with her family is prevalent in various intuitive ways throughout any given day. When off leash, Penny has an innate understanding of acceptable behavior that she abides by. She also forestalls the arrival of her dog walker and easily reads the emotional state of each family member, knowing when and who needs the most comfort. Penny has different energetic roles with each human family member, too. With her mom, she is a protector and helper for every task. She receives tough love from her sister, affectionate names from her brother, and cuddle time after dinner with her dad. Her parents say, "She adds a loving presence to our lives, a loyal and loving commitment to us and our kids."

Genetic Variations of Goldendoodles

F1—Golden Retriever+Poodle (any size), 50% Golden Retriever, 50% Poodle. Coats are soft and wavy, rarely curly, low to moderate shedding. Very little coat maintenance needed.

F1b—an F1 Goldendoodle bred back to a Poodle, 25% Golden, 75% Poodle. These are the most hypoallergenic coats—little to no shedding. These dogs are usually curly coated, occasionally wavy, and do need to have their coats cut/groomed periodically.

F2—F1 Goldendoodle + F1 Goldendoodle, 50% Golden Retriever, 50% Poodle. The more curly coated F2s will have low shedding, while the straighter Golden Retriever–looking coats will look like a Golden Retriever with less shedding. These dogs can be a little smaller than the F1s.

F2b—This is an F1 bred to an F1b, 37.5% Golden Retriever and 62.5% Poodle. These dogs are similar to the F1b but have just a little more golden retriever in their looks and personality.

F3—Any other mix of breeds is referred to as F3 or multigen.

"Until one has loved an animal a part of one's soul remains unawakened."

—**Anatole France**

Buster

English Cream Golden Retriever | 5 years old

Buster is described as "sensitive, intuitive, and caring," and his actions certainly support that. Without any training, he can anticipate seizures ten minutes before they occur by giving a clear and specific signal of alert beforehand. This came in particularly useful when his human companion was driving and had time to pull over. He also knows when her head is hurting and the days she's on medication, and he will not leave her side for one minute.

Buster has two full-time jobs. During most weekdays, he goes to work at the Americana Manhasset, where he's become the personal shopping mascot and besides having good taste in shoes, he's a calming presence to all those around him. When he's at home, he aims to please by helping out around the house. He can open the refrigerator, take items out, throw things in the garbage, and take laundry out of the dryer.

"I've had a dog in my life since I was born. Never have I had more of a soul connection with a dog as I do with Buster. He anticipates what I need and is there to give it."

Instagram: @buster_couture

Codega

Great Dane | 9 months old

This Great Dane's name means "guide or protector who illuminates the way" from the Codega who protected the citizens of Venice. He lives up to his name, especially when the family takes a walk and he jockeys to take the lead to check out what's in front of the girls, who are seven and nine. His mom says, "Cody has helped to fill the spaces left by loved ones who are not around anymore. He gets off the couch to greet each family member who comes into the house. After a tough day, it's great to have that type of hello." This is the first pet for the girls, and, according to their mom, it has already been beneficial to them because Cody "is more like a furry younger brother who needs attention, who wants to play with them and wants to be included. They have learned to check his needs, like water and food, and now make sure that they do some 'Cody-time' when they first walk in the house."

Cody's juvenile manner is present in his keen ability to go for items that his family doesn't want him to play with such as slippers, socks, tissues, and stuffed animals. This usually ends when they have to chase him around the kitchen and bedroom to extract and retrieve these items. His mom adds, "Cody has not really gone after books, except some Irish ones that I inherited from my father. My Italian American husband loved the fact that our German dog, with an Italian name, went after my Irish books."

Dora

Long-haired Dachshund | 5 years old

Dora is a dynamic companion to her eighty-year-old human. There is no dog walker. They take two to three daily walks on the streets of New York City together where Dora likes to, as her human says, "perimerate" by walking only on the edge of the sidewalks. "I don't know why she does that! I also don't know what motivates her to move through the apartment from place to place or why she has different moods each day. I do try to figure her out, though." The mental and physical tasks they offer each other seem to keep them both in healthy form.

She was named after Dora the Explorer, but only *after* she was named did her companion experience several chance encounters related to that show. One year, the writer of *Dora the Explorer* rented her summer beach house. Another year at a dog park, she relayed the story of Dora's name to a stranger, only to be told that she was actually talking to Dora herself. "I am Dora!" the woman exclaimed. "The show was created about me!"

Throughout the day, Dora hears how beautiful she is and what a good girl she is from her loving companion, who lives alone with her. She feels that one of the perks of having a dog is how it helps with her social life. "In general, people are much friendlier when you have a dog. I've met some very nice people while walking Dora. Some have become my good friends."

Socializing, mental stimulation, decrease in stress, companionship, and protection are all ways that dogs can enrich the mind, body, spirit, and space of the elderly.

Monty
Soft-Coated Wheaten Terrier | 8.5 years old

Enzo
Soft-Coated Wheaten Terrier | 1.5 years old

Monty was part of a litter all named after Shakespearean characters; he was Montague and his sister was Capulet. His family kept the name because they felt it was appropriately regal. He was already groomed in true Wheaten style, with his beard and fringe in front of his eyes, but the moniker gave a nod to his young, energetic spirit. His favorite place to hang is on the cool, marble floor in the bathroom, which his family calls "Monty's summer home." He has a sweet demeanor but can also be a diligent guardian of the house. His mom says, "He will come over while we are watching television and put his head on the couch to be scratched. If you ask him if he wants 'tummy,' he'll drop where he is and roll over." His family has noticed that not only will he sit close and "make you feel warm and safe" to whoever is upset, but he will continually keep his eyes on them.

When Monty and parents went to the breeders looking for another Wheaten, a thirteen-week-old Enzo spotted them from across a clearing and came prancing over "like he knew we were his new family," they said. Enzo can leap off the ground with all four paws in the air—his parents call it the Classic Wheaten Greet'n! Enzo is a super high-energy pup, except when someone in the house is not feeling well. When that occurs, he becomes noticeably calmer and will put his paws on the bed and his face in his loved one's face, checking in on them regularly. When there's hugs happening, he'll want to get in on that action, but if there's arguing, he stays away. Besides dutifully assessing loved ones' moods and health, Monty and Enzo enjoy spending their days running around the yard, going to a stimulating play group four days a week, and taking long weekend walks.

Chester

Papillon | 12 years old

Chester was a gift from my mom—twenty-two years *after* she passed away," says his human companion. "My niece called me from Greece, urging me to go to the North Shore Animal League. She was adamant that I go. I was so tired and didn't want to, but went anyway and didn't see anything. As I was leaving, I saw a lady in a white coat walking a Papillon who was just groomed. She told me that someone was coming back for him. I waited for over three hours, and, thank goodness, no one returned for him and I got him!" Staring affectionately at him weeks after, she suddenly realized why Chester was so special. She always associated butterflies with her mom and believes that her niece was the vehicle to push her toward this dog with the long, fringed, wing-like ears, whose French name means "butterfly."

Chester is clear about what he likes and doesn't like. He doesn't like to kiss, and he doesn't like to be groomed, but he enjoys drinking milk at ten o'clock every night, and if you forget, he will bark to remind you. There is only one toy—out of a basket of thirty—that he prefers to play with every day. He gets walked four to five times per day, understands Greek, and likes to give high-fives when prompted. His human companion loves how "he lovingly gazes into my eyes. He's truly a gift from my mom."

Every dog in our life comes to us for a reason. Maybe your dog has taught you the values of patience, the rewards of caretaking, or the deeper meaning of compassion. It's helpful to reflect on why we have been drawn to certain dogs and the lessons we've also learned about ourselves through their unconditional love. For tips on how to intuitively connect with your dog, go to: *Spirit: Eileen Garfinkel, Animal Communicator Interview,* on page 251.

Dawkey

Boxer | 7 years old

When Dad comes home, he gives Dawkey the most enthusiastic greeting out of all the family members. Dawkey already knew he was near from the sound of his Mustang coming down the street, so Dawkey was ready and waiting by the door to greet him and then engage in his favorite pastime of "rough" play.

Although he loves Dad, he spends most of his time alone with Mom. She's the one who walks him most often and provides his care. "I am not a chronic hugger/patter/demonstrative type, but I think he is aware that I love him," she says. She gives Dawkey a bone almost daily. "Problem is that I keep them in the freezer. So every time I open the freezer, he starts licking his chops. I've gotten to the point that I wait 'til he's not around before I open it!" Both Mom and Dad agree, "He is a warm and comforting presence in our home."

Casey
Labradoodle | 6 years old

Rex
F1b Goldendoodle | 3 years old

Rex is a Goldendoodle, which is a hybrid resulting from a Poodle and a Golden Retriever (for more on the genetic variations of this breed, go to page 19). Casey is a Labradoodle, which is a cross between a Labrador Retriever and a Poodle. Both are known as a "breed-in-progress" because it's still too early to be considered a purebred with assured temperament traits and predictable characteristics. That said, both the Labradors and Retrievers are known to be sociable, eager to please, and gentle dogs, while Poodles are known for their intelligence and problem-solving skills. These amalgams often create an ideal family pet, and that's exactly how this Winnetka, Illinois, family feels about theirs.

With two sons of the household off to college, Rex and Casey have developed a strong connection with the youngest son, rushing on command to his bedroom every morning to wake him and every evening to say goodnight. Each claims their own designated spot on his bed. "They are his comfort when he is sad and joy when he is happy," says their mom.

Casey is described as an "incredibly sweet spirit—with a host of health issues." Her Addison's disease (a malfunction of the adrenal glands) requires her to receive daily medications and injections every three weeks at the vet. The latter is something she oddly looks forward to with such delight. Her mom says, "She whines and squirms in the car when she realizes we're going and runs in when we get there. The vet techs all love her and come out to greet her when she's there. She runs up and greets each of them like long-lost friends. When we go into the exam room, she jumps up on the table before they can lower it for her and stands patiently to get her shot."

Rex can sometimes be a bit nervous and anxious, but he "masks it with a tough-guy exterior that evaporates when someone challenges him." He likes to stick close underfoot and will knock you with his paw if you have stopped paying attention to him. Together, Casey and Rex like to wrestle with each other and wait patiently at the door for their mom until she comes home.

This rare breed has survived two near extinctions and comes in two varieties: long coat or smooth.

Honey

Russian Toy | 6 years old

Honey was my savior at a very difficult period of my life. When I was in the room with him for the first time, he seemed to sense that I needed him. He went around several other people, climbed on my lap, and went to sleep. We have been together since. He is a true emotional companion, and I have never felt unconditional love until I found Honey," declares his mom.

Honey's mom and dad often joke that he has telepathic abilities. He seems to be intuitively drawn to whoever needs his tender attention most. When friends come over, he picks up on who is most stressed or upset and will sit with them "for as long as it takes," says his mom. Then they report feeling much better afterward. "He senses when I am at my saddest or happiest and always acts accordingly. When I sleep, Honey acts as if he were watching over me. He faces outward and alerts me to any noise, protecting me," says his mom.

Dad says, "Honey is a softy, a bundle of fun and work! There are many times when Honey has sensed our distress and he would just squeeze himself into our arms! There is something soothing in his presence that almost instantly takes the edge off and provides unbelievable comfort." When Mom and Dad are home together, Honey can't choose who to sit close to. He goes back and forth between the two, corralling them together, "running this passage back and forth," says Mom, until the two of them are sitting close to each other with Honey comfortably in the middle. "If I am upset, he will follow my every move and will climb and sit on my lap or my chest so that I could hold him and cuddle him. If I am angry, he senses that, as well. In fact, I use him as my personal barometer to see if I should cool off and take a deep breath, because he would move away from me only if I would speak with an angry, loud voice."

Simba

English Cream Golden Retriever | 8.5 years old

Simba is a highly trained Seeing Eye® dog with an intelligence that, at times, must override his own primordial canine instincts when the safety and well-being of his companion are at stake. When well-intentioned strangers stroke him, he can't react. When an off-leash dog gets up in his face, he must remain calm. When an unexpected cyclist comes out of nowhere, Simba uses "intelligent disobedience" in anticipating the trajectory of the bike while overriding his handler's command to stop her from impending danger. At that time, she will know that something is amiss and use her senses to tune in to the environment. Simba is constantly assessing obstacles on the ground as well as the height and width of where he is guiding his companion to ensure she can safely walk through the chaotic and often unpredictable streets of New York City. When he must relieve himself, it's on an exacting schedule, and if circumstances alter the call of nature, he knows to gently guide his companion off to the side in a particular way.

"When he is working, please don't pet him," pleads his legally blind companion. What most people don't realize is that when you touch a Seeing Eye® dog—even when they are resting—you are distracting them from doing their jobs. You are taking away the confidence, dignity, and independence that come from the complete and focused dynamic required of them at all times. "People who try to give him food or people who are texting while walking create difficulties for me, especially other dogs that come near him. He's taught not to react, but if another dog comes too close—friendly or aggressive—it's a real problem."

As hard-working as Simba is, his life is not all business. "Simba knows that when his harness comes off, that's when he can play and be a dog! At home, he'll grab a toy, kiss me, and be silly." Harness off, home together, Simba will put his head on her shoulder and hold tight. There have only been two times they have been separated. "Twice, he had to go overnight to the vet. Being without him made me feel naked." There is not a day that goes by that she does not feel grateful for Simba. "The fact that he does this because he loves me and I love him is an amazing surprise."

Simba and the Seeing Eye

Simba came from the nonprofit organization The Seeing Eye® in Morristown, New Jersey. Their spokesperson, Michelle Barlak, states that after birth, "volunteers hold them who have hats, glasses, strollers, or canes to help them avoid any phobias. Vacuums are regularly used near them, and CDs with sirens, construction and traffic sounds, thunderstorms, and loud noises are played often to help desensitize them against such sensory experiences." At seven weeks, they go to live with a volunteer family where they learn the basics of obedience, and then they go back to the facility between 13 and 16 months old for their formal training that goes on for months 14 through 17. Afterward, they're matched with an owner based on their "pace and pull," since—like people—each dog has a natural walking cadence and some owners may need more or less pull or a faster or slower pace.

The Seeing Eye® is not government funded, relies solely on donations, and is one of the only organizations that allows every blind person to own their dog, unlike others who loan them. This way, it enables the recipient to have assurance and dignity knowing they own the dog and it can't be taken away because it's on loan. The Seeing Eye® only asks for a $150 fee for the first dog (and $50 for each dog thereafter). They place approximately 250 dogs per year with an estimated cost of $65,000 per dog in breeding, raising, and training. Barlak implores other dog owners to keep their dogs away from service dogs, stating, "Even people who think, 'Oh, my dog is friendly and would love to say hello to this working dog,' don't realize that when these service dogs get attention from strangers or other dogs, it builds up to future distraction issues where service dogs want to interact regularly with other people or dogs." In addition, when passing a service dog with your dog, always try to walk on the opposite side of the sidewalk. If you can't catch your unleashed dog running toward a service dog, you must warn the owner so that they can be prepared for this incoming bothersome distraction and are able to help their dog refocus. "These dogs are not perfect; they are animals that, as much as they have been trained, might react to certain distractions that can be problematic to its owner," says Barlak.

Believe it or not, Simba and his blind handler—and many others who are visually impaired and have seeing eye dogs—still get turned away from stores and businesses that are ignorant of the laws and the Americans with Disabilities Act, which allow them to go into any privately owned business that serves the public. Other blind people in those situations usually call the police, but as The Seeing Eye® advocacy specialist, Ginger Kutsch shares, "Sometimes you just want to join your family in the restaurant for the birthday party, and instead you have to wait an hour outside before the police show up."

To donate or learn more, please go to www.SeeingEye.org

Zero

Greyhound | 3 years old

Greyhounds are known for three specific traits: they're the fastest breed, they're not big barkers, and they often "lean" to show their affection. Zero leans. A lot. "It's funny to see—like he's standing at a 45-degree angle. And if you back away, he will adjust to edge up against you again," says his mom, who found him through Greyhound Friends of New Jersey (www.GreyhoundFriendsNJ.org), a nonprofit organization that finds homes for retired racers.

Zero's entry into their lives was very serendipitous. "After our first greyhound, Dash, died, we started looking for another on the Internet. On one website, my husband spotted Zero—short for Zero Dark Thirty—and mentioned learning more about him. I called, and, coincidentally, they told us they had one particularly nice dog—out of many—for us to meet." It was Zero. They knew before they went to go meet him that he was theirs.

"Greyhounds aren't what you'd call critical thinkers. They are literally born to run. They are the jocks. That said, about three months after adopting Zero, something in the way he moved around the house, reacted to us, and got into a groove signaled that he had figured out that he had a whole new life, that he had a home." In adjusting to his new life off the track, he had to *learn* to play and is still in the discovery stages of how to get a squeak out of a toy. "Zero fills the house with spirit and fun. He gives a big boost to all who live here," says his family. Now that's something to lean into.

Artwork: *Landscape Series*, acrylic on canvas, Luc Leestemaker.

Charlie

Cockapoo | 2 years old

Charlie's first walk of the day is to his companion's office, where he likes to stay under her desk—or on top of the conference table during meetings. "He can be playing with other dogs in my office and I won't know where he is, but I'll get up to go to the bathroom, and he will come rushing over like, 'Oh my

God, I thought you were leaving without me.' He never goes far at all!" says his mom.

At home, "he creates the feeling of family and togetherness, helps us relax, and also adds more purpose to my days." In addition to that, he knows when to be protective. When he's inside by himself and his mom arrives outside the door, he won't bark. However, when she's inside alone with him and he hears a noise outside the door, he will.

"I am with him most hours of the day, so we know each other better than most dog-human duos. He follows me everywhere. He's my sidekick, and any chance I have to take him places, I will bring him."

Instagram: @adogintheapple

Benefits of Dogs in the Workplace

Nearly 1 in 5 American companies today allow dogs in the workplace.[1] Studies[2] have shown that dog-friendly offices tend to be more productive and have employees with lower blood pressure and stress levels. Opportunities for exercise and socialization, as well as an increase in employee morale and satisfaction, create a wellness contribution that significantly enhances company well-being. Also, employees might work longer hours, rather than worry that they have to get home right away to their dog.

---

1   According to the American Pet Products Manufacturers Association
2   *International Journal of Workplace Health Management*

Cooper

Labrador Mix | 7 years old

Atrip to a local shelter for a "small" dog resulted in seeing only loud, barking dogs, standing up. Except one. "We asked the man there why this one was just lying there and if we could see him. When he opened up the cage, Cooper stood up and we could see why. He only had three legs," says his human. So they went into another room to get acquainted, and when he sat cross-legged on the floor, seventy-pound Cooper sat in his lap. The bonds of love and loyalty were born.

Cooper was a stray who had been hit by a car. He was malnourished, his stitches were infected, and he had worms, but in his loving home, he healed and flourished. He learned to do most things other dogs can do but has difficulty with uncarpeted stairs. One night, a fire alarm in their apartment building went off, so his dad carried him down ten flights of stairs and back up again. Cooper loves walks but cannot go the distance a normal dog can and will often need to take rest breaks. He also doesn't have the balance a four-legged dog has. He cannot jump, and his family has never tried to let him swim. Since he cannot scratch himself on the side without the leg, when he is itchy, his hip makes the rotation action as if he were doing it, and his mom will know to scratch his neck or the back of his ear. Sometimes on the couch while watching television, his mom will massage his muscular, overworked back leg. Cooper always shows his appreciation for the scratches and massages afterward.

Six years, two kids, and a new suburban home later, Cooper likes to spend time in the open yard but will never stray. He has become quite protective and close to the children, letting them do whatever they want to him. He prefers to walk in front of them during strolls so he can evaluate all who come close. The adoration is mutual. "We try to do everything together," his dad says, adding, "We bring him with us wherever possible and tailor vacations around him. He brings us such joy."

"A dog lives in the moment and always hopes for the best." —**Unknown**

Mantequilla
Rhodesian Ridgeback | 8 years old

Chiquita
Puggle (Pug and Beagle) | 4 years old

The front yard is their favorite space to be every day, whether they find themselves in the middle of one of Chicago's harshest winters or soaking up the glorious summer sun. They relax and watch the heavily traversed road. "People all around town tell me they love seeing them sitting outside, enjoying life!" says their mom.

Mante can be slightly aloof, yet he fills his family with reassuring love that he delivers by quietly sitting close. He's named after the Spanish word for butter, since he's been known to silently pilfer a stick from the kitchen counter. Chiquita is a diminutive power house of vigor who can play all day long. "There are times when Quita just plain ole has more energy, and she jumps to and from as Mante sits majestically staring at her—or more likely staring in the opposite direction," reveals their mom. When Quita doesn't have a playmate available, she'll throw the ball up in the air to play catch by herself. When she finally tires out at night, she *always* waits for Mante to first get into bed, and then she will nestle in next to him as they curl into a yin/yang symbol for the night. How does this ninety-pound big boy show his love for his tiny pal? Mom says, "Sometimes Mante just opens his mouth and puts Quita's entire head into it, and he gnaws softly on her head."

Daisy

King Charles Cavalier | 16 years old

After it was decided that the family wanted to get a King Cavalier, one serendipitous event after another brought Daisy and her family together. "A friend suggested we look into this breed, which was unfamiliar to us. A few days later, we saw one on an *Animal Planet* dog show and thought it was beautiful. The next day, we were walking the boardwalk, and I told my sister how we wanted to get a King Cavalier but I wasn't sure how to find a reputable breeder." As luck would have it, right then a woman came walking toward them with a Cavalier and told them about a trustworthy breeder in the area they should contact. When they called the breeder, they learned that every pup was spoken for in the upcoming litter. They were disappointed but knew they had to be patient. A few weeks later, they were overjoyed when told that one family had changed their minds. After an interview process, Daisy was theirs!

"Four or five months after getting Daisy, my sister went to Arizona and saw a tarot card reader who was very accurate with her life and personal issues. My sister told me that the tarot reader went on to talk about me and how I was married with two children, and she was very certain she saw a recent female energy in my life and a bond of pure love." Her sister was a bit confused at first, and the tarot reader—convinced that she was accurate—pressed her further. "Oh, my God! It's Daisy the dog!" she exclaimed. She was right. Her bond with Daisy was a pure channel of love that continued to grow deeper into the next decade.

When both kids left for college, Daisy would go into their rooms and check for them. Daisy's family feels that she was a source of calm in their home and that just sitting and petting her relaxed them all. When sitting on the couch, every family member has received The Cavalier Mugging, which involved Daisy jumping up on their laps, puting her front paws on each of their shoulders, and pressing her body against theirs.

At sixteen, roles have changed. She was once the companion and comforter, but she had lost her hearing and her sight had become limited. The family had to become *her* companion and comforter. She taught the children of the family about "responsibility, putting another's needs first, and unconditional love. We are so grateful to her." The day after this photograph was taken, Daisy passed away.

For help with dealing with the loss of a pet, go to Spirit: Wendy Van de Poll, Canine Bereavement Specialist Interview, page 261.

"Dogs' lives are too short. Their only fault, really." —Agnes Sligh Turnbull

Basenjis are from central Africa and are known for being a "barkless" dog due to their unusually shaped larynx.

Sonya

Basenji Mix | 9.5 years old

Sonya can cleverly open any door while in a closed room, likes to hide her bones in between the sofa cushions, and doesn't particularly like men with beards, men with walking sticks, or men in uniforms! Sonya was found at an ASPCA sidewalk adoption event. Her future family was walking by with no intention of getting a dog, but one look at her, and she came home with them immediately. Just as they "saved" her, Sonya tries to do the same with them. If a family member is lying on the floor and she believes they're hurt, she will take them by the shirt and try to drag them to safety. "She is my soul mate and is always at my side," says her mom.

"Oddly, my dogs are color-coordinated with the fabrics and wood stains in my house. Browns, blacks, tans, whites. They look absolutely charming wherever they plop down in the home," says their mom.

Alfie
Chihuahua/Pomeranian Mix | 4 Years Old

Kevin
Shih Tzu/Bichon Mix | 5 Years Old

When it's bedtime, Mom says to Alfie, "Do you want to go to bed?" and he flies off the couch and runs to the front door to go relieve himself. Then, he runs up the stairs and waits for Kevin, who has to get carried out. Kevin's not physically restricted, "he's just lazy," says their mom. Mom reports that when asked if they want to go "bye-bye in the car," Alfie will lose his mind and hysterically run to the door and wait for her. Kevin will do the same but not as excitedly—unless the names of the kids are mentioned. "Then he will look toward the door and lose it," says his amused mom.

Kevin sits up on two legs like a human, putting his elbow up on the couch to relax. "He's funny, and nothing ruffles his feathers," says his family. He has a special connection to the youngest daughter of the family, who personally chose him when he was a pup. When an infant visitor came to the house for the weekend, Kevin never left the baby's side. He even stayed outside the closed door while the baby napped. Alfie gets along with everyone, too, except for his twenty-six-year-old brother, who discovered that Alfie does not like his back paws touched, yet he does it anyway to "get a rise out of him." Alfie growls at him.

"Continuous effort—not strength or intelligence—is the key to unlocking our potential." —Winston S. Churchill

Max

Maltipoo | 10 years old

Max's journey began as a puppy in a popular pet store where his human mother found him. "Although the pet store owner claimed all of her dogs were from reputable breeders, Max had health problems from the get-go. There is no doubt in my mind that he was from a puppy mill, and, for that reason, I consider him a rescue dog."

Max has hemophilia and has suffered four internal hemorrhages. His first was in his spinal cord when he was two, compressing his discs so that he was unable to use his hind legs. After surgery and a lengthy recovery using front and back harnesses, he was able to learn to walk, run, and jump again. His third hemorrhage was the worst, and when he failed to respond to transfusions, the veterinarian delivered the news that Max would not survive. Max has an indomitable spirit and a determined and feisty disposition—he rallied more than ever and survived.

"Although I know he's a dog, I often feel like he's my son from another mother," says his dedicated mom. Max reciprocated the devotion when she had to undergo a second round of breast cancer surgery and radiation. Max never left her side and always remained quiet, calm, and present. "He's always following me around. If he's not following me around, he's looking at me!" she says.

This past year, Max hemorrhaged again. Because of the expenses and uncertainty of the outcome, operating was not an option, and the veterinarian was not confident Max would regain the use of his back legs. Since he always seemed to far outlive anyone's expectations, his family decided to view his disability through a positive lens and focus on what he could do versus what he was unable to do. With his harness, Max would walk for a mile and play inside and out, and the family would also do their own physical therapy exercises with him. Sure enough, Max continued to defy all odds and started walking two weeks before this photograph was taken. His family says, "The outpouring of support when he was paralyzed and the unbridled expressions of surprise, joy, and even tears from the friends and strangers we see on our daily walks is remarkable."

Duke

Boxer/Pit Bull Mix | 6 years old

After being rescued from a kill shelter at four months by New York City firefighters, Duke found his loving home in a busy Brownsville firehouse. Duke knows the drill when a call comes in. He doesn't shy away from the loud sirens; he moves away from the moving trucks and doesn't leave the apparatus floor when the doors are up. His favorite places to sit are *on top* of the chief's car during roll call and on a chair at the kitchen table, surrounded by his human buddies. If food is left on the table and a call comes in, as tempting as it may be, Duke knows not to eat it.

His connections to the firefighters run deep at this multiunit firehouse, which houses Ladder 120, Engine 231, and Battalion 44. "Duke definitely has his favorite people here, and when they come in to work, he gives them a longer, extra enthusiastic greeting," says one firefighter. "But when any of us return from vacation, we get a more excited welcome back greeting, too. He knows each one of us."

That connection is not necessarily determined by who gives him the most food, but by who "spends the most time with him and gives him the most attention." He's managed to turn even the most ardent non-dog lovers into devoted friends and often goes home with various firefighters, joining them on family vacations, and is always at the annual company picnic. While at one firefighter's home, Duke had a treadmill mishap and lost his tail. Duke's expenses come out of the collective pockets of the firefighters. After the photo shoot for this book, Duke's Facebook page (DukeFDNY) was active with concerned firefighter posts of how his big photo shoot went that day, jokingly questioning if he'd still be an appealing photogenic subject for this book with a shortened tail.

"We have stressful jobs," says one of his main handlers. "We often deal with demanding and traumatic events, and having a firehouse dog can help alleviate those stressors."

Muppet's family says, "She can read our moods and is alert to what our needs are—whether it's a quiet approach or enthusiastic joy! Her spirit energizes us."

Muppet

Shih Tzu Mix | 4 years old

After rescuing Muppet when she was three years old, her new family felt that she was eager to belong with them. Muppet enthusiastically learned commands to impress them, but as far as playing went, well, that was an activity she had to be *taught*.

"She seemed so sad. We brought in an animal behaviorist to evaluate her and to show how to unlock her personality." After some more research online, within one day, Muppet was playing!

For more on Canine Behavior tips go to Mind: Dr. Megan Maxwell, Canine Behaviorist Expert Interview, on page 149.

Hide-and-Seek with Your Dog

Daily mental and physical stimulation is vital for your dog's well-being. Mixing it up beyond fetch can be both rewarding for you and your pet. While your dog is in another room, hunker down in a hiding place—inside a closet, crouching down in the tub, standing behind the curtain—then call him or her. When they find you, give lots of praise or a treat!

*"I have found that when you are deeply troubled there are things
you get from the silent devoted companionship of a dog that
you can get from no other source."* —Doris Day

Buddy

Beagle Mix | 12 years old

Everybody loves Buddy. He is exceptionally gentle and calm and has soulful eyes. Even neighbors' dogs who don't like other dogs get along with Buddy. Little children love him because he does not jump or lick, and he tolerates poking, rough petting, tail pulling, and lifting of his feet without protest. Even a deer from the nearby woods likes to play with Buddy because he doesn't bark or chase her. "He does not force himself on anyone—his sign of love is a light sniffing of faces," says his adoring family.

What does Buddy love? Food. He is completely food-motivated. His mother always has cereal for breakfast and would get up from the table to go to the bathroom. "I would be surprised I had eaten as much as I had. One day I came back in and saw Buddy sitting on my chair, face in my bowl! He had been eating my cereal when I left while leaving the spoon perfectly in place!" He even figured out how to open a drawer and pull out food, so the family moved the goods to a higher cabinet. Buddy then jumped up on the bench below the cabinet, opened the door, and jumped up to the shelf where his food was, pulled it down, and ate an entire bag before they got home. That cabinet now has a rubber band around the handle. Many times, he has jumped up and pulled down bags of bread and consumed it all. His family has had to take him to the animal emergency center three times for eating rib bones and an entire loaf of bread.

Besides food, he does have a soft spot for his family. A pet camera revealed that he howls for them after they leave and will scratch at the doorframe. He'll also tend to them when they're sick and even placed his paw on his mom's knee and lay with her after her knee surgery.

Hard to believe that such a gentle fella would have been abandoned, but that's what happened to Buddy before he was adopted. Buddy was found on the cold, Chicago streets in January when he was eight years old. "For the first couple of weeks we had him, he always walked with his tail down. I knew he finally trusted he had a loving, forever home when his tail was up and he would bark at dogs walking by. Until that time, I don't think he thought of our home as his territory. He wants to be with someone all the time—he has to be wherever we are."

Stella
Xoloitzcuintli | 4 years old

Venus
Xoloitzcuintli | 11 years old

Poppy
Chihuahua | 10 years old

Truman
Chinese Crested Mix | 3 years old

Stella, Venus, Poppy, and Truman are all considered "special needs" dogs by their human mother, who is dedicated to giving them each a great deal of love, attention, and diligent health care. Stella struggles with epilepsy and visual impairments. After Hurricane Sandy, when Stella was found clinging to a floating ottoman while her home was severely flooded, she has had difficulty walking on terra firma, or solid earth, ever since.

Venus was rescued from a breeder who lost interest in her when she didn't pan out as a "show dog." Poppy is an abnormally tiny Chihuahua weighing in at 40 ounces who battled through chemotherapy and suffers from allergies and inflamed airways, which bring on continuous breathing problems. According to her mom, "A diet of wild salmon and microgreens along with acupuncture treatments have saved her life." They've become a deeply bonded pack with Truman, the only male, taking on the role as guardian and ringleader—while he works through his own extreme anxiety disorders since being found on the freeway of Los Angeles. Each dog has a special position and placement in the bed that never changes. When Poppy stops breathing at night, Truman will wake up Mom so she can assist her, and then Poppy rallies on. "We are all deeply bonded and interdependent. We live and breathe for one another."

Truman is the only male of the pack.

Venus's breed is pronounced Show-low-its-queen-tli.

"The pack has its complex dynamics, but Stella and Poppy are always very sweet together," says their mom.

Cooper

English Setter | 6 months old

When Cooper's mom went to the breeder to choose a puppy, the selection process was over the minute Cooper climbed into her lap and looked into her eyes. She felt they were meant for each other. Afterward, the breeder informed her that Cooper was deaf in one ear. This news reinforced her fated choice even more. Her youngest son, who was with her, is also deaf in one ear. She was already in tune with the needs and sensitivities of living with a loved one with hearing loss.

Cooper came into her life at a pivotal turning point after she left decades of a grueling and demanding corporate job behind. "He brought me balance, fun, and good karma. He livened up my home and made it a much more spirited environment," says his mom. At only six months old, Cooper amazes her with his intelligence. "The dog walker comes between 10 a.m. and 10:15 a.m. If she's late, at 10:30, he will get the leash in his mouth by himself and wait at the door!"

Hearing-Impaired Dogs

Dogs with white spotted coats such as English Setters, Dalmatians, Bull Terriers, and Whippets[3] are among the breeds at the highest risk for congenital hearing loss in one or both ears. The lack of pigment cells in the inner ear causes nerve endings to die off in the puppy's first few weeks. If your dog is deaf, make sure that his or her nametag includes Deaf. Stamp your feet before waking your dog and use hand signals for training.

---

3 WebMD Pet Health, *Training and Caring for a Deaf Dog* Feature by Sandy Eckstein http://pets.webmd.com/dogs/features/training-and-caring-for-a-deaf-dog

Sunny

Mixed Breed | 5 years old

When her family found her, Sunny had been in an animal shelter for all four months of her life. She was in a kennel with another dog that kept pushing her out of the way. After this happened several times, Sunny moved away from the other dog, sat down, and made eye contact with her new, soon-to-be family, who felt she was saying, "I'm here if you want to pet me." As soon as she was in the car heading to her new home and life, she curled up in a ball, sighed, relaxed, and has since always seemed to have an essence of gratitude toward her family. "She says thank you with her eyes all the time, gives lots of licks and cuddles, and likes to stay close," says her human mother, who adds, "She is constantly checking my expressions. If I smile, she smiles. If I'm confused, she looks quizzical. It's really quite funny."

Besides her friendliness to every dog she meets, her most marked characteristic is her impressive dexterity with her paws. She easily opens doors to let herself out. Some doors have had to be changed out for ones with more complex knobs because she hasn't quite mastered how to *close* the door behind her.

Sunny enjoys a raw diet, occasional bones to clean her teeth, and an active and healthy lifestyle that includes beach walks and play dates. Her wellness care incorporates probiotics, herbal remedies to address everything from eye problems to tick prevention, and The Holistic Home Company Calm Dog spray and Paw Balm. Her family reveals, "Sunny completes us and has a special bond with each member. Her friendly disposition and playful demeanor add to our happy environment and encourage us not to take life so seriously."

Artwork: *The Constant Rumble of Waves*, oil on canvas, Stephen Brehm.

Chanel

English Bulldog | 4 years old

Chanel is a muscular, stout lady who likes to grunt and lounge near the fireplace. When the family watches television, she's always near them, wrapped in a blanket. At night, she won't lie down in the bed until the covers are pulled back for her. Her favorite activity is playing with sticks in the garden that are ten times bigger than she is and running as fast as her short, stocky legs will take her!

Bulldogs are not known for their swimming abilities, but for their independence and self-sufficient manner. However, they do need assistance with breeding, since their body type makes it tricky and awkward.

Wrigley

Light Golden Retriever | 10 years old

Wrigley follows hand commands—even though his family never taught them to him. He sits when they place one hand on their chest, and he stays in place when a hand is held in a "stop" position. He's also adept at patiently communicating his needs. When Wrigley needs to go out, he will stand in front of the door and make a little crying sound. When it's dinnertime right at five o'clock, he will look for his mom in the house, and when he finds her, he stares into her eyes, giving a little cry. When she grabs her keys and purse, he observes, tilting his head to one side, questioning if he will be allowed to come, while eagerly awaiting the right hand signal.

Wrigley plays a different role for each family member. For her son, his role is loyal playmate. Wrigley has an after-school routine of waiting for him on a certain rug to receive a back rub while "talking" to him about his day. His dad spoils him, and his mom has an instinctual, maternal connection. She says, "If I feel sad, or angry, he will follow me from room to room, never leaving my side until I tell him, 'It's okay.' When we're happy and laughing, he will do something like grab a shoe and run around with it. He only carries it; he will not eat it. It's like he wants to join in the fun!"

Jem

West Highland Terrier "Westie" | 4 years old

Jem understands when told that it's "television time" and will immediately head into the TV room and sit on the couch. As soon as he sees a suitcase or cooler, he knows its time for a trip, and he'll bark until he's assured that he's going, too. He can also anticipate—by the tear of the package—when it's time for his insulin shot. Jem will never forget who has given him treats or has done him favors.

His family describes him as stubborn and lovable. In a typical terrier manner, if he doesn't feel like responding to "come," he simply won't move. When his family returns home, he gets on his hind legs and jumps up and down. "He has a face and dark eyes full of pathos. You can't help but want to take care of him," they say.

Angie Girl
Silky Yorkshire Terrier | 12 years old

Rosie Bones
Black Labrador | 4 years old

A trip to the pet store was scheduled to help soothe the aftermath of a breakup. When newspapers started moving around in what looked like an empty pet store cage, Angie Girl was discovered. "I think back to her demeanor as a baby hiding under the newspapers while all the other puppies in other crates jumped around and barked," says her mom. "She was nervous and shaking and hid her face in my arms. Once she calmed down, she looked up at me and licked my hand. I was in love." Together they both healed, and she says, "Angie Girl taught me what commitment is."

Eight years later, married and not having luck having a child, Rosie entered as a new member of the household. "Rosie helped my husband and me fill a void—the lack of having a child—that was good for our mind and our spirit. It also filled the void we were feeling—it gave us a project, to love this dog and give her a fabulous life." Rosie and Angie Girl hit it off swimmingly. Every morning, Rosie licks and grooms Angie's face. They snuggle together on a chair in the living room and share a bed at night. Three years passed, and after mom learned she was finally expecting a child, Rosie would often sniff her pregnant belly. After the birth, Rosie became dedicated to baby, and the two have developed a strong bond.

Dylan

English Cocker Spaniel | 7 years old

Dylan likes his routines. In the afternoon, he drags out his blanket to the living room or to the garden to cuddle and sniff. In the evening, he receives a treat at 8 p.m., and if you forget, he will make sure to remind you. When his family is not home, he will wait patiently for them by the door. "We love him to bits. He provides warmth and unconditional love," they say.

Smokey

Poodle/Sheltie Mix | 8 years old

Shading of gray fur from pale to charcoal is Smokey's most notable physical trait, but his inner persona is not quite as obvious. Smokey likes to take the soles out of only certain family members' shoes, and, while walking along the Hudson River, he will mysteriously and suddenly jump wildly. These behaviors keep the family entertained. "He softens us and makes us laugh," says his mom, "particularly when he lies down in his seal pose"—which is another mystery to appreciate.

"We long for an affection altogether ignorant of our faults. Heaven has accorded this to us in the uncritical canine attachment." —George Eliot

Artwork: *Paul and Ranger*, oil on canvas, Paul Richard.

Tate

English Cream Golden Retriever | 1 year old

Tate is a dog who naturally touches many lives. He has an affinity for the elderly, the handicapped, and the homeless. If he happens to cross paths with someone in a wheelchair, he will pull toward them and rest his head in their lap. He's not free with kisses unless you are elderly—then he won't stop. If you're homeless, he will make a point to pause, make eye contact, and connect with you. Because he loves to roll over on the city streets and expose his stomach to strangers to rub, this often draws a crowd of hands on him, which one time led a woman to rush over in a panic, concerned that Tate was injured and in need of CPR. He doesn't only connect to humans, though. Tate will let small dogs climb on him like a jungle gym, roll around for hours nibbling lips with his girlfriend, Ginger, and play for hours with his lake buddy, Logan.

While in Whiskers Holistic Pet Store (see Whiskers' interview, page 188), a stranger came up to Tate, bent down, held Tate's head in his hands, and was overcome by emotion. "It's okay," reassured the observing cashier, "he's a pet shaman." The shaman looked up with tears in his eyes and said, "You're a very blessed person to have this dog in your life. He's an amazing dog." His companion couldn't agree more. The love and kindness that Tate provides to all comes right back to him in abundance.

Tate has a charmed life with a minimum two-hour daily walk to start the day wherever he is—whether it's a walk along the East River, on the beach in Cape Cod, or a on lake property in New Hampshire. At his home base in New York City, after he runs with a pack of Goldens at Central Park, he attends the School For The Dogs (see School For The Dogs interview, page 158) for four hours a day with one-on-one play and training time. His healthcare regimen includes chiropractic work, acupuncture, organic oils, and homemade organic meals, which contain probiotics, glucosamine, and immune system–boosting powders. Essential oils and homeopathic pellets are used to ward off fleas and ticks, and he regularly sees a holistic vet.

Says his devoted human companion, "Tate is not a pet. He is a soul mate. He gets me."

Instagram: @tatertotnyc

Rugby

(Most likely) Spaniel/Irish Setter/Golden Retriever Mix | 14 months old

Rugby has an extraordinary obsession for bugs. His mom says, "If I ask him, 'Where's the bug?' he goes nuts looking for one. He'll go to extremes to get it and eat it. Even if it's just a mark on the wall and not a real bug, he'll climb sofas and tables to get to it—sometimes to our dismay!" She has even asked Rugby to get certain bugs that she did not want to get herself.

Soon after a car hit the family's previous dog, they decided to get another. Rugby was in the first shelter they went to, and the workers there called him their "Rasta Dog" because of his distinct crimped hair, which stands up on the top of his head. They played with him but ruled him out because they were hoping for a hypoallergenic dog. They went to other shelters, saw possible options, but couldn't all agree. After four visits back to the first shelter, they realized they were drawn to Rugby. Surprisingly, they were talked out of adopting him by the shelter. They were told he was "not ready and that he was on a training regimen due to resource guarding." The family was not daunted by this news. "We had a very natural connection to him. We do feel he was meant to be ours!"

From his previous life as a stray to now indulging in morning games of rigorous fetch, evening neighborhood walks, a weekly seven-mile run, and five-mile walks at a nature preserve on the weekends, Rugby has settled into his new life quite well. Each family member engages in different activities with him, carving out special time either to sit together at an outdoor café or go on long car rides. As far as "resource guarding" is concerned, his family says they can approach his bowl and even take things right out of his mouth, and he's fine with it.

Tips When Getting a Dog from a Shelter

- Always ask how the dog ended up in the shelter.
- Ask to take the dog for a walk. It's a good way to get to know their demeanor and if they need more training.
- Does he or she have any special medical needs?
- Does the dog get along with other dogs? Pets? Children?
- Is this dog housebroken?

Charlie

Schnauzer/Terrier Mix | 7 years old

Charlie's most distinctive feature is one ear that stands up halfway. He had an ear infection a couple of years ago that caused him to flap his ear around so hard, he broke a blood vessel, which caused a hematoma to form. When it was drained, it was wrapped in an ace bandage for a month, and afterward, the ear remained at half-mast. Charlie is calm, responsive, and always interested in what's going on in the home. His mom says, "When I smile at him or look at him intently, he walks to me or wags his tail."

Charlie seems to anticipate when events are about to happen that he does not like. This includes taking the vacuum or dish detergent out, as well as when his mom reaches into a cabinet for his shampoo because he's not fond of taking baths and will then hide. He's also not crazy about dogs with short hair, except for Labradors. But what he does love are his girls. Charlie was discovered on an adoption website by his two human sisters, who were in seventh and eighth grade at the time. He slept under their beds and would always hang out near them. When they went off to college, he missed them terribly. His mom works from home and says, "As a single mom with an empty nest, I have welcomed his presence. It has also provided a connection to the way life was when my girls were at home. When they return over the holidays, he is beside himself."

(L to R): Toro Jones, Molly, Ruby, Davey, Norma Jean

Ruby
**Mixed Shepherd |
13 years old**

Norma Jean
**Pit/ Boxer Mix |
12 years old**

Davey
**Pit/Bulldog Mix |
11 years old**

Toro Jones
Pit/Sharpei Mix | 6 years old

Molly
Pit/Labrador Mix | 2 years old

Ruby is the "old maid" of the group. Before she got to the household, she was stressed and thin, but after joining the group, she nearly doubled her weight. Norma Jean is the "lover" and cries to meet other dogs she sees on the street. Norma had been the previous alpha of the then-quartet, but when Molly entered the band, Molly let each member know that she was the leader and in charge. Like the others in the house, Molly came with a sad story. Her parents were told by the adoption event workers that she was "detached and deaf." This mushy cuddler soon proved that she was neither. Toro was bypassed at adoption events, too, because he had no hair. After joining the family, his mange went away, and now he has a full coat that he likes to have groomed by Norma and Davey. Davey is the group protector, was the first member of the herd, and doesn't like when his humans get ready to leave the house. When they recently returned from vacation, while the other dogs were ecstatic, Davey was miffed and ignored his parents for a while.

The best part of a five-dog household? "It's the insanity of it, and when you see them all sleeping on top of one another at night. You just don't have that dynamic when you have one dog or even two—the dynamic is completely different with five. They compete for food, they compete for warmth, they compete for love, but in a very loving, caring way, just as children do. If we had a big enough bowl, they could all eat out of the same one without incident. And yes, our house smells like dog, but I love it."

Chaka

Yorkshire Terrier | 11 years old

At five pounds, Chaka is tiny, but her character and heart are mighty. She lives for Jamaican food and has a special penchant for curry chicken. Chaka relates and interacts to each family member differently by mirroring their personality traits. Her mom is the tender center of Chaka's universe, and Chaka continually stays by her side, offering love and comfort. She approaches her laid-back brother coolly, and with her sister, she is tauntingly playful, stealing her underwear and then leaving them around the house.

With her dad, Chaka preferred to act like a tiger and would friskily play. She would innately know when he would be coming home from work, even though the times would usually vary. She'd perk up, hop up on the couch by the window, and look for him. After three minutes of sitting there, her mom would then know to open the front door, and she'd see him walking down the street. When he suddenly passed away three years ago, Chaka became depressed and lost her energetic vigor. Even offers of walks and treats couldn't get her out of bed or away from his shoes, where she constantly hunkered down. "She just seemed so sad and acted like a totally different dog," said her mom. Chaka then amped up her support assistance to the family and would stay with whichever family member was in the most distress that night. Her mom says, "Chaka has reminded me that pets are sentient beings with a little soul, and she has given me the broader understanding and appreciation for another life form."

Chaka has a talent for opening all the doors in the house by using her "signature move" of scratching, pushing, and throwing all her weight into the door. It worked great every time except when she inadvertently got stuck in a closet for several hours while her family put up LOST posters with her picture throughout the neighborhood.

Gracie
Golden Retriever | 5 years old

Ellie
Golden Retriever | 12 years old

Gracie is a puppy at heart. "She even looks, feels, and smells 'puppy-like' and loves to drape herself on a lap or be held like a baby," says her mom. Her companion, Ellie, takes the role of calm, canine matriarch of the house and is described by her mom as "the grande dame of the home." Ellie is subdued, aloof, and patient. She is often found sitting in the front hall of her London home, leaning up against the wall, "looking like she is holding up the house—physically and metaphorically." Her mom reflects on Ellie's aloofness by offering, "Ellie is much less physically demonstrative than Gracie, [but] somehow she doesn't seem any less emotionally giving." The two are pals and are hardly far apart from each other. "Gracie and Ellie are the soul of our home. Their unconditional love is the emotional bedrock of anywhere we are."

Monty

Goldendoodle | 1.5 years old

Monty is veritable proof of how a dog can change your life. "I would do anything for Monty," says his dad. "I am not a morning person, and yet every weekend I get up before 7 a.m. just to take him to the park. We've changed vacation plans to ensure we don't need to fly and can drive with Monty. We even got a bigger car just to fit our dog." Monty sure needs the room. This crossbreed of Poodle and Golden Retriever is five and a half feet tall when standing on his hind legs. He can even knock food off the top of the refrigerator—in addition to stealthily opening book bag zippers to eat lunch leftovers.

Monty's previous owner gave away this cute pup because another pet in their family was becoming jealous of him. "Due to his overwhelming cuteness and desire for attention, I can see how that may arise, but it's a grievance for it to be a reason to surrender a puppy," says his dad. Monty loves to join in on hugs when he sees them happening and can also provide hugs on command when someone taps their chest with both hands. His parents provide lots of mind and body stimulation that includes four walks per day, off-leash time at the park, doggie day care twice a week, meetups with other doggie friends, and on occasion, he goes into work. His mom says, "Monty is very attached to us, our family members, and his very close human friends. He will jump up, spin around, and just go crazy. He really shows his love for the ones who care about him."

He likes nearly everyone, although mechanics and skateboarders are not his preferred company. "He's a giant furball for us to love . . . a living shag rug," say his parents. "We have a mutual, unconditional love for each other. We treat him like a child, and he truly is a part of the family."

Instagram: @montydoodledoo

Lou Lou

French Bulldog | 2 years old

At only two years old, it's quite amazing the amount of tricks that Lou Lou can do on command: retrieve slippers, drop dead when she hears "BANG!", lie down and roll over several times, jump on different beds when asked, and find five or six of her toys hidden around the house. She knows neighbors' names and their dogs' names, too, and will pull you toward their house when she is told she is going to visit them. She loves going to "day camp" once a week, and on the morning of, she feels frustrated with the shorter walk, but once she is told that she has camp, she hurries back, will barely eat her breakfast, and will go downstairs to eagerly wait to be picked up.

Lou Lou loves being dragged along the grass by her leash so her back gets "massaged" on the ground. Her mom says, "This has alarmed many people who think she is being tortured and threaten to call the ASPCA!" Her most marked physical characteristics are her big ears and svelte body. She's very friendly to people and other dogs but most partial to large male dogs.

"She *is* the atmosphere of my home. It would not be complete without her," says her mother. "Her mere presence brings joy." And just like her scattered toys around the house, her essence is everywhere.

Ollie
**Nova Scotia Duck Tolling
Retriever | 13 years old**

Penny
**Nova Scotia Duck Tolling
Retriever | 1 year old**

When the kids were desperate to get a dog, they brought a book of dogs to their dad. He chose a breed he thought would be impossible for them to find in England—a Nova Scotia Duck Tolling Retriever. As luck would have it, there was a breeder nearby, and that began their love for this unique, ginger breed created to lure and retrieve waterfowl.

Ollie's family feels she has a sixth sense of knowing when and whom to comfort. She will stick close, offering unwavering silent support during times of grief or stress. Penny's energy is a bit more nervous and playful and filled with quirky behavior, like when she gets scared of baby strollers or sculptures of animals. But her endless vigor has brought out a sense of playfulness for Ollie as well as the whole family. Together, this white-pawed duo creates a sense of balance within the household and also within the lives of their loved ones.

Riley

Welsh Springer Spaniel | 7 years old

If I leave the house for ten minutes, I will come back to a dog that is just as excited as if he hadn't seen me in a year!" exclaims his mom, who will sometimes hide in the house when Riley is out for a walk. "He searches the whole house for me and is so excited to find me!" While his welcome receptions may be enthusiastic, his anticipation of good-byes are heartbreaking. He senses trips before they occur, and when the suitcases come out, he will climb into them to protest. When keys, purses, or jackets are grabbed, Riley will head to the door filled with optimism that he might be coming along. One of his favorite places to go is Ollie and Penny's house. The trio are great friends and often hang together. His loved ones all agree, "He always makes coming home welcoming. It is so lonely when he is not there."

Thor

Corgi | 4 months old

After seven years of "being tortured by the family to get a dog," Mom acquiesced. However, agreeing on a breed was the next challenge. Mom loved mini Dachshunds. Dad loved Golden Retrievers. Neither would budge. "The distance between the two was immense," says Mom, "but when the family was on a white water rafting trip and collectively decided that a Corgi would be the chosen breed, we happened to see one on the side of the river and took it as a sign."

Back home, waiting lists for Corgi pups as long as three hundred deep felt discouraging, but a year later, a Colorado breeder sent eight-week-old Thor—the only survivor from his litter—on a plane to his new family. At the airport, the kids cried and hugged him. His mom says, "He kind of brings the family together more, because instead of the kids being up in their rooms, we are all together around Thor." Even his name was a communal pursuit. He was named after the nickname for the family's favorite Mets pitcher, Noah Syndergaard.

Having a puppy can certainly be a challenge. Right now, he's on a ten-walk-a-day regimen, a trainer comes once a week to help sort out his "unruly phase," and his mom can't wait until he grows out of nibbling everything around him. "It's like a third baby!"

Humphrey Bogart (Bogie)
Schnoodle | 8 years old

Lauren Bacall (Cally)
Maltipoo | 8 years old

Bogie came first. His mom says, "He was the little red runt of the litter who kept pawing at my leg while I was set on adopting a white puppy who kept running away from me. Papers were signed. Then my sister's words came into my mind: *'Don't pick the one you think is the cutest. Tomorrow they will look different. Pick the one that wants you.'* Paperwork was changed. Bogie came home with me." Neither of them has regretted that last-minute decision for a single moment.

Cally was abandoned and found in a field by some boys who could not keep her. She was hungry and dirty. They brought her to the groomer where Bogie happened to be getting groomed. Cally ended up going home with Bogie and family that day while attempts were made to locate Cally's family. Every night at bedtime, Bogie was asked if he thought they should keep Cally. He barked enthusiastically. They all bonded. But then three months later, the groomer called to say that he found Cally's owner. Relief set in when his next sentence was "She said you can keep her!"

Often, dogs' quirks are what can make them so oddly endearing. Bogie does extensive leg extensions when he pees, loves to hump his five-foot teddy bear, and howls at emergency sirens. Cally is a food thief who ate an entire plate of spanakopita and was only caught because of the spinach in her teeth. Alone in the kitchen, she climbs from a bench to a table to get onto the counter, where she looks for open food in the upper cabinets. She will be first at the front door for greetings but will then back away so that Bogie will receive most of the affection. They both love being read to. They are also incredibly entertaining and become the center of attention when guests are over.

Both dogs haven't changed much since they were puppies. Bogie will still paw at his human mother's foot like he did when he first met her. Cally will bark at Bogie when he's out of line. Having known deprivation, she continually reminds Bogie how good they have it.

Sedona

Siberian Husky/German Shepard Mix | 11 years old

Sedona's soon-to-be mom vowed to wait one year after her previous dog, Lovely, passed away before getting a new one. On the exact one-year anniversary, she was oddly pushed out the front door by her cat, Max. "Max is a highly intuitive cat who was exhibiting the same behavior he did on the day I got my previous dog,

Lovely. He woke me up at 6 a.m. and pushed, and pushed, and pushed me out the door to go find her. The message that Max was giving me for my new dog was, 'Go out onto the streets, Mommy. You will find the dog on the street. She is really close to the house. Go now, Mommy. Go now. Today!'"

So off she went, walking around the neighborhood, looking for her new dog, thinking the whole thing was crazy. Meanwhile, Lovely's dog walker was nearby. He had been very close to Lovely and, that day, had suddenly felt a divine presence from above of Lovely's spirit passing through him just as he passed by a dog day care and adoption facility. He had never felt anything like that before or since. He went in, saw Sedona, and told them to hold her while he got the dog's new owner. He then waited in the lobby of her building, and, when she arrived, they both shared their stories. Then off she went, only two blocks away to get her dog.

Sedona easily made herself at home, settling in without any fuss, enhancing the home with peace and calm. She gets four walks per day, two hours off-leash in Central Park, and a three-hour pack walk with her friends. She is also treated to massages by Kim Freeman. *(For massage tips, go to Body: Kim Freeman, Certified Canine Massage Therapist Interview, page 192.)* Every day, she gives kisses to three household cats for whom she often gives up her bed. She became a certified therapy dog, helping children with learning disabilities read, and often demonstrates tender moments with infants and children she comes across.

One day, as Sedona's mom was working alone in a friend's pet store, a man and woman entered the store. Sedona had been soundly sleeping, but when they walked in, she was on sudden alert and would not allow her mom to pass by her to get near the couple. Five minutes went by with Sedona showing her teeth and staring them down. The man asked if the dog was hers. She said yes. They apologized for disturbing her dog and left. The next day, they learned that the same couple robbed several convenience stores. "She is my hero," says Sedona's mom.

Chief

Cavapoo | 7 years old

Cavapoos (also known as Cavadoddles) are a combination of a Cavalier King Charles Spaniel and a Poodle. This crossbreed is known for its playful disposition and companionship, and that is exactly what Chief's family likes best about him. They enjoy watching television together because Chief ardently looks for dogs and then whimpers when they leave the screen. The family also relishes watching him run. "He prances! Run, leap, run, leap!"

His favorite spot is in the window. He's been known to wait for up to three hours there when he knows the dog sitter is on the way. He also watches out for squirrels and has proudly brought them to the back door on occasion.

He likes to cuddle close, loves to lick, and will "coo" when he's held. His loving and lively energy is much appreciated by his family. "He brings so much joy to the family and home. He is always happy and wanting to be where the family is."

Dexter

Chocolate Labradoodle | 5 years old

Dexter is known for his specific relationships with each human member of his family. His mother is the one he listens to the most. With his father, he is playful and also likes to climb up on the couch behind him—not next to him, but behind him! He's great pals with the three sons of the family whom he adores and with whom he has particular habits. The grandmas treat Dexter just like their other grandsons, and he is most excited to see his grandpa, who always walks him when he visits.

Dexter runs to sit and wait by the stairs when he sees jackets being put on or hears talk in the house about going out. He prefers hanging with people more than other dogs and has an endearing habit of "rubbing his nose on our knees," says his family. "He makes the home feel warmer and is always ready for a hug, to celebrate, or to cry with."

Harley
Cavapoo (Cavalier Spaniel and Poodle) | 6 years old

Cody
Cavalier Spaniel | 5 years old

Layla
French Bulldog | 8 months old

Cody likes watching dog shows on television. Harley will paw you at 8 a.m. and 8 p.m. to seek affection. Layla will make sure you see her going to the bathroom because she knows she will receive a treat. All three love this ottoman and are usually found piled up all together on top of it.

Birdy
(Most Likely) Glen of Imal Terrier | 5.5 years old

Boscoe
Kerry Blue Terrier | 10.5 years old

Birdy's family describes her as "pure love, sweet, expressive, and content." Birdy came to her family "with broken wings . . . we also had broken wings and heart from our three previous dog losses over six months." They had to teach her what toys and a dog bed were. They named her Birdy because they wanted her (and themselves) to heal and to spread their wings again.

Birdy has the unusual and quirky habit of sitting up like a person all day long! If she's in the car, she'll sit upright and rest her arm on the ledge. Her family says that she has probably run away from the circus. Yet they describe Boscoe, with his silvery blue coat and skin, as the funny one. "Boscoe has an amazing sense of time. He knows the exact time of day for walks and will often sit and wait at the window and bark if one of us is late," say his parents. Just don't bring out the luggage. It makes Boscoe so sad, he vomits.

Clay

Golden Retriever | 6 years old

Clay likes to listen to heartbeats. He will jump into your lap, look into your eyes, and listen closely. He was bred to be a service dog by Honor Golden's in North Carolina. (Honor Golden's Therapy & Assistance Dogs is an accredited, nonprofit organization that provides special Golden Retrievers to veterans, special needs individuals, and service organizations, as well as family pets.)

Although he was brought into the family as a loving pet, he made it very clear from the time he was a pup that he needed a purpose. He soon found that calling by being involved with his mom's biofeedback client sessions wherein she trained the minds of high-performance athletes to reach their peak functioning levels. Clay helps them find their stillness through meditation and visualization. She paid attention to Clay's nonverbal cues and soon discovered it seemed to be a gift as well as an innate part of his personality and desire—as well as the receptivity of her clients—when he joined them in her studio. "He simply enjoys being of service by means of offering comfort," she says.

Many of the athletes she works with are Type-A, and Clay teaches them what it feels like to find the calmness within and then to carry that into their sport to perform their best. Simply put, they "integrate Clay" into their performances.

Clay comes to all the sessions unless a client has allergies. The exception is when she meets clients at their own homes, on the field, or in group workshops. He begins offering his assistance by immediately sitting or lying very close to her clients while she speaks with them, or often he sits directly in front of them, looking into their eyes and lying next to them when they meditate. His presence immediately evokes a desire to be close and a shared calmness. When a client lies down to meditate, he often will put his head on their chest so he can hear their heartbeat, which fosters a very powerful client-Clay connection. There has never been a client who didn't want him there. They all respond that his calmness is a "real service" and "quite unusual compared to any other dog they have known."

Every day he swims at the dog beach, runs alongside a bike, and has two long walks. He is under the care of both a holistic and a traditional vet who balance out his care. As far as his obsession with listening to heartbeats of those he feels close to is concerned, his mom says, "He came to us this way as a pup. I think maybe he had a very comforting mom who did this with their pups, and he has kept the tradition alive." What she knows for sure is that "Clay rounds out our own hearts with his unconditional love. He just gives, wanting nothing in return."

Moose
Chocolate Labrador/Hound Mix | 9 years old

Ginger
Yellow Labrador | 14 years old

Moose provides comic relief while also being the chief security officer of the house. His favorite spot is the third or fourth step on the stairs, which keeps him perfectly positioned to be on guard and monitor all outside activity. He had a sketchy history that began with an unpleasant home and two rescues, which may explain his enigmatic dislike for certain men and children. His parents describe him as "very intelligent. He is quick to learn the difference between good and bad behavior. Although he struggles with actually choosing the good behavior in some cases . . ."

Ginger's dainty feet led to being named after Ginger Rogers. She has a penchant for stealing napkins off of laps—which her dad admits makes dinner parties a challenge—and has even snatched small handbags. Her brother, Moose, is loyal and protective of her, "although she of him, not so much," say their parents. "We think she enjoys the companionship of Moose, but she is not as playful with him as he wants to be with her. She's the queen and knows it."

They each have their own beds, and they prefer different rooms. Ginger is independent, relies on no one, and can be quite vocal about her needs if she wants something. Ginger came to them when she was three years old from a retiring couple who wanted to focus more on traveling. So they took her for a trial walk, and when they came back, Ginger's toys, dish, and bed were sitting next to their car. "She was a sweet dog and we knew we could give her a good home, so off she went with us!"

Rhodie

Miniature F1B Goldendoodle | 4.5 years old

Rhodie is a great example of how the "right" dog often finds us. Rhodie's mom had her heart firmly set on the red male she was planning to pick up from the breeder, but when this small, red, curly, female pup climbed into her lap and looked into her eyes, she *knew* this was the one, and their instant bond was formed. When Rhodie returns to her apartment building after a walk, she knows if her mom has already arrived home from work. "I don't know if it's my perfume or something, but she'll run to the lobby elevator, wait anxiously, then tear down the hallway and scratch at the door to get to me," she says.

Rhodie is equally close with her dad, with whom she plays a bit rougher. She falls asleep on his chest and likes to "chopstick" with him (cuddle between his lower legs). At night, Rhodie knows she can count on a treat, but if Mom forgets, she will sit in the kitchen looking repeatedly between her and the treat cabinet. Before bed, they practice a calming ritual of a belly rub and a loving, deep look into Rhodie's eyes. "It's nice to have a few private moments with her, quietly communicating our love!" she says.

Rhodie makes their home a happy place full of love. "My husband and I always put her needs above our own and want the best for her. We are constantly laughing at things she does and 'oohing and aahing' at how cute she can be. Our apartment has turned into a crazy playpen at times and is definitely prepping us for when we expand our family beyond just our four-legged love one day."

For *Ways a Dog Can Prepare You For Parenthood* go to page 113.

Instagram: @littleredrhodie

Ollie's favorite place to sit is on this front lawn Adirondack chair, hoping he can greet or play with anyone who walks by.

Ollie

Cockapoo | 18 months old

Before finding Ollie, the family had a single goal of bringing home a "gentle" dog. They found a mild-mannered eleven-week-old puppy whose "Cocker Spaniel body on long Poodle legs" was exactly what they were hoping for. Ollie is loving and loyal with a family member who suffers from Parkinson's, will lie down in front of children, passively defer to aggressive dogs, and will wait uncomplainingly for his family to wake up in the morning so he can be let out.

Ollie's owner says, "He has been great for getting me out of the house, giving me structure, getting exercise, and connecting with other people. I also feel that when I sit with him, I have a sense of mindfulness as I look at the world and nature at a slower pace, through his eyes." In addition, her levels of necessary thyroid medication have decreased since welcoming Ollie into their family.

Ways a Dog Can Prepare You for Parenthood

- Responsibility for another living being.
- You care deeply for their well-being.
- You pick up their poop.
- You have to discipline them.
- They bring out your parental instincts.
- They depend on you for everything.
- They teach you how to put someone else first.
- Feeding and care of a dog can be expensive.

Winnie

Cockapoo | 2 years old

Winnie likes to find socks and then hide them all over the house. Some nights, she'll bring those socks as well as treats and toys to her human mom in bed. Winnie enjoys a steady balance of healthy food, and lots of exercise and socialization with other dogs and people.

She intuitively seems to know when her mom comes home from work because that's when she moves to the couch and waits, looking out the window in anticipation of her arrival. "She is very adept at reading emotions and loves to cuddle right up to you," says her mom, who walks her three times a day at the beach, in the woods, and along the Illinois Green Bay Trail. She believes that by letting her be a free dog off-leash on occasion, she's a happier dog.

Maxine

French Bulldog | 4 years old

Maxine sometimes barks at nothing while seemingly looking at something that isn't there. Her parents call it "Seeing spirits!" She enjoys lots of daily walks around the city during the week and long hikes in the country on the weekends. "She looks up at me when we walk or hike to make sure I am still there. It makes me smile," says her dad. At the end of the day, when she sees the movements of bedtime preparations, she will come trotting into the bedroom with a bone to nibble for a bit before getting into her crate for the night. Her fathers say they love her "wacky and friendly personality and that she makes the home more alive and joyous."

When left alone, a web cam reveals how this mischievous team will pull only hardcover books off the bookshelf. Wally pulls off the spines and Birdy rips up the pages.

Birdie
(most likely) Yorkshire Terrier/Maltese Mix | 12 years old

Wally
Old English Sheepdog/Poodle Mix | 3.5 years old

Birdie was rescued from a grim, puppy-mill life filled with abuse and bred for multiple litters. After her new prospective family was interviewed by the shelter, hosted a house visit, and supplied many references, Birdie was matched with them. "She took a long time to adjust to my husband," says her mom, who attributes the hesitation to Birdie's previous mistreatment. "It's taken over five years, and she is still normalizing. Her anxiety has gotten better since Wally has come onboard." When there are certain situations such as travel, company, or thunderstorms, they are both given Bach Rescue Remedy. "I put a few drops in their water and it may be more my thinking that it helps, but it does seem to calm Birdie down," says their mom. She adds, "The Thundershirt works wonderfully, too. During hurricanes a few years back, I put the shirts on them, and there was an immediate change in behavior. Birdie goes from 'Holy crap! What is happening?' to 'I think I will just sit down and yawn.'" *(For more on Bach Flower Remedies and antianxiety canine compression shirts, go to Spirit: Sarah Hauser, Animal Reiki Expert Interview, page 241.)*

Wally is hefty and mellow, and Birdie is petite and skittish, yet the two are best friends who balance each other out in many ways. Birdie's favorite pastime is watching videos on a smartphone—but never a television—and Wally loves to hike and snowmobile through Vermont. The duo garners lots of laughs when walked together due to the disparity in proportion. Even though Wally weighs five times more than Birdy, they both think they're the same size. Occasionally, they will tussle over toys and bones and Birdie will get a bite in here and there, while Wally just takes it and looks at his parents as if to say, "Did you see that?"

Daniel
Greyhound | 6 years old

Zoey
Black Lab/Blue Tick Coon Hound
Mix | 7 years old

Zoey was found at Abandoned Pet Rescue (apr.rescuegroups.org) when she was nine months old and quite ill. After falling into the pool, destroying walls and crates—anything that confined her—her parents called for a neurological examination, which showed she had a misplaced liver shunt. Instead of filtering pollutants, the shunt was dumping toxins back into her system, "making it seem like she was drunk and agitated," say her attentive parents. After surgery, holistic therapies, and a raw food diet, she was like a new dog—loving and grateful and always with a happy, wagging tail. Her parents are just as appreciative. "She creates all things positive by just making us laugh. Laughter makes a happy, loving home."

Daniel came from Holly Dogs Greyhound Adoption in southern Florida (www. Hollydogs.org), which is a nonprofit organization dedicated to saving retired racing greyhounds who otherwise would have been destroyed. Daniel's battle scars from years at the track are still visible, but his loving, loyal, and sweet nature is his most marked characteristic. When Daniel's mom first saw him at Hollydogs, he walked up to her and started kissing her face. Having had three previous greyhounds who didn't do this, she had always hoped for one who would and took it as sign. Daniel went home with her that day.

Daniel and Zoey are best buddies. They sleep near each other and go for at least two walks together per day when they're not busy protecting the house. Both eat a raw diet and tackle flea and tick prevention from the inside out using quassia bark

powder and black walnut extract. They have found acupuncture to be helpful in strengthening their legs and back.

Zoey has since passed away, just a few months after these photographs were taken. She developed an oral cancer of the soft palate, which spread quickly throughout her body. Although her time on earth was short, she brought great joy and happiness to everyone she met. Her parents have very recently adopted a new girl named Nala, an eight-month-old Chocolate Labrador with boundless energy and endless curiosity who came to them from Labrador Retriever Rescue of Florida. While they can never replace Zoey, they take comfort in knowing that she had a good life, and they have given a chance to another deserving rescue dog.

For help with dealing with the loss of a pet, go to Spirit: Wendy Van de Poll, Canine Bereavement Specialist Interview, page 261.

The cruel and inhumane racing of greyhounds is still active in Iowa, Arkansas, West Virginia, Alabama, and Florida, where thousands of dogs are registered to race.[4] These dogs are often stored in cages that are too small, fed meat from diseased or dying livestock,[5] and pumped with steroids and cocaine,[6] and many suffer broken legs and backs or collapse from heat exhaustion. When they don't win or are no longer profitable in this industry, they are often killed—unless they can make their way to racing rescue organizations.

---

4   According to GREY2KUSA National Fact Sheet, in 2013, 10,657 individual dogs were registered to race.

5   Linda L. Blythe et al., *Care of the Racing and Retired Greyhound* (Topeka: American Greyhound Council Inc., 2007), 151

6   "About Dog Racing: State Rulings," Grey2kusa.org, (Somerville MA: GREY2K USA, 2012)

Baci

Mixed Breed | 6 years old

Pesto

Spaniel Mix | 8 years old

On this hot, summer day in Atlanta for Baci and Pesto's photo shoot, Pesto was a bit forlorn because her favorite swimming spot—the hot tub spa—was out of commission. She watched her dark-furred pal, Baci, do her usual routine of swimming in rapid circles in the pool while yelping, blowing bubbles, and looking like an otter. Finally, Pesto joined her for a quick dip and then rubbed herself on the rosemary bush when she got out. They love the yard and are often found eating blueberries, figs, and raspberries right off the bushes.

Both came from the local humane society. Baci first caught her parents' attention because she was blowing bubbles in her water bowl—a practice she now does all

Pesto likes to throw her bowl when her family is late to feed her or simply when she is hungry.

the time in the pool. The only people Baci doesn't like are yard workers holding equipment. She gets herself in a barking tizzy when she sees them, but Pesto likes them and will try to harness her ferocity by herding her away from them.

The two definitely work together as a team—whether it's playful hijinks or vigilant stewards of the house. For low-level alert issues like the arrival of another family member or an open door, they both approach their human and "stand quietly in front of me, communicating by the way they look at me," says their mom, but for safety issues, they will bark. The duo seem to have an innate sense of fairness, knowing how many treats the other has received as well as a deep concern for the other's well-being. When Baci had a scratched cornea and was in the midst of an uncomfortable veterinarian exam, as usual Pesto tried to intervene and reach her on the exam table to make it all better.

Rookie

Yorkie/Maltese "Morkie" | 9 years old

Rookie reveals his intelligence to his family in numerous ways: he hides under the table as soon as he's told he's getting his medicine. When riding around Vancouver, he gets himself ready and positioned to exit when the car reverses into a parking space. He also has a knack for the finer things in life, like how he will choose only cashmere blankets to curl up on.

Rookie's "three buttons" for eyes and a nose are what melted the hearts of his parents, who first saw him in a photograph and thought he looked like a mini Old English Sheepdog. They love how cuddly he is, and his mom says, "If I'm sick, he never leaves my side."

Most dog owners report that their dogs will stay by their side if they are sick. Research has shown that a dog's extraordinary sense of smell (100,000 times stronger than humans) can detect volatile organic compounds that can indicate disease and sickness. The combination of changes in bodily scents, daily routines, and even facial expressions are all factors that dogs are highly attuned to with their loved ones. What a dog does next with this information brings up the question of canine empathy. Countless under-the-weather dog owners report that their dogs will choose not to bother them as much for play or walks and will want to offer comfort and physical closeness.

Shep
Collie/German Shepherd Mix | 9 years old

Calypso
Vizsla/German Shepherd Mix | 1.5 years old

Teva
Black Labrador | 11 years old

Teva means "nature" in Hebrew. As a puppy, she crawled into her soon-to-be dad's lap when the rest of the litter was running around. She has never met a dog she didn't like, and even when she was viciously attacked, she went back to her attacker and rolled on her back and wagged her tail. Her mom says, "Teva has an equal love for all of us. She gets up when any one family member leaves or arrives."

When Teva was one year old, Shep came into the family. "We never trained Shep. He learned everything from his sister, Teva. Heeling, rolling over, coming when called. He even learned things that I didn't realize we were teaching. When he's walking off-leash and would run ahead, I would say 'Wait for us,' and he would stop, stand, and wait until we reached him."

Shep was not thrilled when Calypso entered the picture when another family member came home from college. When she's around, he refuses to play and will pout. His mom says, "Since [my daughter's dog] Calypso has joined the family, Shep won't fetch if she's around. He will get the ball and run halfway back, dropping the ball away from me so Calypso can't get the next throw." The dogs are trained to stay downstairs at all times. When mom comes downstairs, the doggies clamor for her attention. Clever Shep runs away, grabs a toy, and then shoves it in the other dogs' faces so they will take it to go play and he can have his mom all to himself.

Dogs can help enhance health and well-being with obliging walks and socialization, but Teva and Shep's mom didn't anticipate they'd be responsible for getting her to quit her diet cola habit. "Our dogs go to their cages if we leave. We don't lock them but did when they were puppies, so they still go there. I realized one day that I got a diet cola from the drink fridge every time I would drive somewhere. They started going to their cages when I opened the fridge door. That was when I realized I drank too much diet cola and gave it up!"

"Once you have had a wonderful dog, a life without one, is a life diminished." —Dean Koontz

Harley

Golden Retriever | 13 years old

Nothing stops Harley from seeking out unattended candy and treats. She will climb on tables, unwrap cellophane, and leave a trail of lollypop sticks and wrappers behind, feeling no remorse and a contented stomach. From rooms away, she knows the difference between the sound of a food wrapper that doesn't interest her—like yogurt—and ones that do, such as turkey and cheese. Her insatiable desire for food is equaled by her need for affection. "She loves to be petted and adored more than any other dog I've known. Whatever affection you give is never enough," says her mom, who adds "even if I am playing the piano, she will repeatedly nose my wrist so I will stop playing and pet her!"

Five years ago, Harley was having a regular annual checkup when the vet noticed that she had a hard mass in her abdomen. She had been acting normally and appeared symptom-free. The doctor found a ten-pound benign mass in her chest, which was the largest mass the vet had ever removed from any dog in his more than twenty years of practice. She bounced back quickly after this life-changing event and has been healthy since. Later, her mom reflected on what the meaning of this event was and found that it "reinforced my belief that no one in our lives should ever be taken for granted. Harley's life could have been over very quickly, had the vet found a malignant instead of benign tumor. She demonstrated resilience throughout the ordeal."

Toxic Dangers for Dogs

Gum that contains xylitol is a hundred times more toxic to your dog than chocolate. Keep it away from your dog as well as any other types of candy or food that contain this artificial sweetener. If ingested, get your dog to the veterinarian immediately. Raisins, grapes, avocado, alcohol, and dairy products should also be avoided.

Daphne

Standard Poodle | 10.5 years old

Poodles are known for their intelligence, and Daphne proved hers in only the first week at home when, as a puppy, she opened the gate in the kitchen with her mouth and went upstairs to join her parents in their bedroom. The spot she chose that night on the bed, right between her mom and dad, has been her favorite place to be since. But before she nestles in for the night, Daphne maintains nightly routines. She will patrol the house, opening up each door with her nose, making sure everyone is in their bed before she goes to bed herself. If a family member is not home yet, she will wait at the front door for them.

Daphne likes her own personal space, prefers people over dogs, and is not fond of German Shepherds. She gets sad and quiet before the family leaves on a trip and will begin to pace if there's a change in routine. "We joke that we love her even more than we love one another. She is the baby of the family and very connected to each one of us," says her mom. The connection began as soon as the family went to the breeder when they were about to go forward with adopting a male dog. Suddenly, Daphne jumped up on her dad's lap and nestled her head on his shoulder. She never got down, and that's exactly how they carried her out to the car.

Annabel

Cavapoo | 9 years old

Cavapoos are known to be sweet, easily trainable, and loyal. Annabel demonstrated her loyalty when her mother was recovering from a mastectomy, and she never left her side. Sometimes she is a mild-mannered dog who likes to be picked up a lot. Other times, she shows no hesitation in going after dogs three times her size. Her mom says, "She fills the house with love and makes us stop and enjoy the moment more."

"He is your friend, your partner, your defender, your dog. You are his life, his love, his leader. He will be yours, faithful and true, to the last beat of his heart. You owe it to him to be worthy of such devotion." —Unknown

Tug and Jenny

English Springer Spaniels | 8 years old

Often a two-dog household can be beneficial for the well-being of each canine, offering companionship, security, and a relief from separation anxiety. Tug and Jenny are a brother-sister duo that, in true sibling fashion, demonstrates the typical familial gamut that can range from rivalry one minute to deep affection the next.

Jenny is lively, adventurous, and bold, and the leader of this team. She is a lover of the human touch and has a way of positioning herself near people so that they have no other choice than to pet her neck. She will push Tug away if he's on the receiving end of affection she wants. Afterward, they will run around the house with Jenny playfully nipping at Tug's tail until the duo collapses with their paws around each other or a head on the other's belly.

Tug is sweet, shy, and timid and has a talent for lifting items out of a pocketbook to consume. When he's afraid of getting his feet wet, he looks to Jenny to lead the way. When he's unsure of the snow, he watches Jenny plunge her entire face in, and only then he is poised to give it a try himself. Their dynamics balance each other out and together create a force that their family says bring joy and warmth, "creating a noisy, casual environment" in their home.

Toby

Havanese | 4 years old

Toby will greet you at the door with a toy in his mouth, is known for his sweet disposition, and has an affinity for cats! His mom and dad say, "He never left the side of our two cats, Dolly and Chief, when they died. He stayed with them until the end." Toby will not eat unless his family is eating at the same time. "Toby is the heart of our home. He is the focal point of our attention and affection. He is king!"

"Petting, scratching, and cuddling a dog could be as soothing to the mind and heart as deep meditation and almost as good for the soul as prayer."
—Dean Koontz

Lucy
Unknown Breed | 5 years old

Turbo
Shepherd/Hound/Dachshund Mix | 2 years old

Lucy was six weeks old, homeless, and digging through dumps looking for food on the streets of Haiti when she was rescued. When Lucy arrived in Florida, she was placed on the ground and experienced touching grass for the first time. She didn't know what to make of it and would pick up her paws and shake them off as she walked gingerly. Then, she had her first drink of clean water, real dog food, and a much-needed bath, which she didn't like. "She screamed like we were boiling her in oil!" say her parents.

As grateful as Lucy is for her new, fortunate life, her parents say that she does act quite regal, sitting straight up, crossing her paws, and behaving like the queen of the house. As much as she displays royalty, her mom says that her "street upbringing" will still emerge at times. "I discovered there's a big difference between rescue dogs and street dogs. When Lucy is sound asleep and you startle her, she wakes up and acts very aggressive, even snapping as if to protect her turf."

Turbo came into the mix right after the death of Trep, a shepherd who was very close to Lucy. The loss was devastating to Lucy, who refused to play, eat, or come out of her kennel. After three months, her parents thought a new dog would help get her zest for life back. They found lovable, social Turbo at the local Humane Society. "His size and shape don't match his face! He has the face of a German Shepherd, body of a hound dog, and legs of a dachshund," his adoring mom says. Turbo immediately made himself at home and developed a love for jet skiing with his dad and jumping off the dock. He quickly took to Lucy and would constantly try to get her attention, but it took her a while to warm up to him. Finally, a year later, Lucy has started to play with him.

"We plan things as a family and will often stay home more and entertain just so we don't have to leave them. They are a huge part of our lives. They can read our energy and know when we're happy, sad, playful, or mad. They respond to our feelings. They give 100 percent unconditional love at all times," say their devoted parents.

Someone always stays with Zuzu in the convertible when parked—otherwise she would jump out!

Zuzu

F1B Goldendoodle | 4.5 years old

Zuzu loves when the keys are grabbed because she knows, more often than not, she will be going for a ride and will then wait at the front door. She goes everywhere—shopping, errands, bookstores, and outdoor cafés. She will jump into the front seat and happily pose for strangers when she's in the convertible.

On a cool day, if she's left in the van for a brief minute, she knows how to unlock and open the handle to let herself out.

Her family says, "A lot of dogs associate the car with the vet, therefore, they develop a hatred toward the car, but since we take her so many different fun places, she has only good memories there."

Ever since Zuzu was a puppy, she would vocalize her needs: from thirst to hunger to wanting to go out, Zuzu will clearly let you know what she desires—and usually it's a car ride with her family because it means an adventure right alongside her loved ones.

Car Travel Tips with Your Dog

- To first introduce your dog to car trips, start by letting them explore the car briefly while it's parked and not running. Build up with short trips that end somewhere fun, like a park or field, so they don't just associate the car with only going to the veterinarian.
- Avoid feeding your dog right before. This will help alleviate motion sickness.
- It's best to secure your dog in a harness and seat belt or in a locked-down crate when traveling.
- Don't let your dog stick their head out of the car window. They could get hit by flying objects or get an inner ear or lung infection from the wind and cold.
- Most everyone knows not to leave their dog in the car on a hot day, but did you know that even when it's 60 degrees outside, it's too hot? The inside of the vehicle can heat up to 100 degrees in a matter of minutes.

Artwork: *Day in the Park*, oil on board, David E. Gordon.

Betsy

Bichon | 10 years old

Betsy has strong likes and dislikes, especially when it comes to her fondness for neighborhood boyfriend, Teddy. She will walk right up his driveway and wait at his front door. Her mom shares, "For some reason, she loves Teddy unlike any other dog. She jumps on him and sniffs him and initiates playful chasing. They're all dog behaviors that are normal, but we have *never* seen her doing any of those things before. To this day, he is the only dog she acts that way with. So, I guess there is true love even in the doggy world." Betsy also likes bones and treats but will never eat them—only collect and guard them.

What Betsy doesn't like is the cleaning lady and basically anyone new coming to the house, especially if they go to her bathroom, where she likes to hunker down when she isn't feeling well. (That's why Betsy's leash had to remain on while Susan shot her for this photograph.) Her mom calls her "unpredictable" at times and adds, "She has a split personality. In and around our house, she is very bold and aggressive, almost. Outside our home, she is very docile and meek. People who have seen her in both circumstances have a hard time believing she's the same dog."

Her doting mom injects her with insulin daily for her diabetes and shares that she loves her "tenaciousness—she survived a lot. Whenever I come in after being away from her—even if it was just one hour—she likes me to sit down with her on my lap and reconnect by holding her for a few minutes. When we are outside and she is unsure of the surroundings, she stays very close to my legs. I am her source of comfort and she is mine."

Instagram @betsydiabetesdog

Mulligan

Boxer | 9 years old

Mulligan's nickname is Nurse Mully because he can tell when someone isn't feeling well and will care for them, cuddling close and checking in on them in a gentle way. He adores children and lives for Halloween because he gets to personally greet more than one hundred kids who come to the door. This tender soul does not like it when household members seem upset or raise their voices—even if they're just excitedly relaying a story. In those cases, he'll leave the room.

He smartly distinguishes his boundaries in exacting ways, like when a loved one has work clothes on, he will keep his distance, or if a family member doesn't like their face licked, he will not engage in that favorite pastime of his. His other favorite hobby is helping wash cars. When the bucket comes out, he's ready to go and will get upset if he's left inside.

His family says, "Knowing that he will be there to greet you and unconditionally love you makes the house a real home." Which is summed up perfectly by the sign at his window seat.

Bowie

Labradoodle | 13 weeks old

At just over three months old, the family is still getting to know their blue-eyed, golden puppy, with whom they have already fallen in love. Every day he receives hours of play, exercise, and cuddles from his family, who are discovering that he likes to eat grass and dirt, is able to dribble a soccer ball with his body, and likes to play tug-of-war.

Bowie's mom says, "Bowie has changed the atmosphere in the house. He's brought great joy and liveliness. He's also teaching our kids responsibility." While Bowie may not be aware that he's imparting accountability and duty, he does seem to be cognizant that wherever he goes, he gets lots of "oohs and aahs" for his cuteness.

II
Mind

INSIDE THE CANINE MIND AND BEHAVIOR, THE EXPERT INTERVIEWS

The cross-species bond between dog and human is a unique connection, enriched by a dog's keen observation of loved ones' body movements, tone of voice, smells, and household routines. It's been well documented that the mind of a dog is equivalent to that of a two-and-a-half-year-old, that they do indeed dream and even laugh (it's a sound much like panting). We know that they are capable of emotions such as happiness, fear, depression, anxiety, and jealousy. But when it comes to *what* they are thinking, it is a bit more of a mystery. Canine behaviorist Dr. Megan Maxwell helps shed some light on the inner life of a dog by explaining how they learn, why some dogs don't like each other, why they closely observe our faces, and much more. Sometimes, it just takes one visit from an expert like Maxwell to turn around an issue like anxiety—or in Muppet and Zero's case, to simply be taught *how* to play. Play is a vital aspect in a dog's life. In this section, we learn from dog toy and puzzle inventor Nina Ottosson about why play is so significant to a dog's mental well-being. When dogs like Pepper become experts at their puzzles, Ottosson shares how to continue to engage and challenge to hone their problem-solving skills and tire them out.

Evan MacLean, director of the Arizona Canine Cognition Center, tells us about the beneficial biological effects of bringing your dog to work, like Monty, Charlie, and Rhodie's humans often do. His research shows that just having them in the workplace can make for a sharper and more productive day. The science of canine behavior is not just relegated to the lab, as Annie Grossman, co-owner of School For The Dogs shares; it occurs right in her dog day care and in her training classes, which are "a great way to keep your dog's brain working in ways that will keep them happy and net good manners," not to mention they also learn how to work an iPad!

Perhaps most noteworthy in delving into the mind of the dog is how their intelligence has evolved to coexist with and assist humans. They can be trained to sniff out bombs, cancer, blood sugar levels, and, like Buster, can alert their companion before a seizure occurs. On a daily basis, highly trained Simba guides her companion out of potential danger and is a master of "intelligent disobedience"—overriding commands when she quickly assesses that they would put her companion in harm's way. But don't be discouraged if your pup isn't so much of a heroic working dog, as he or she is most likely a dog of leisure who often amuses you. Often, the simplicity of our dog's unique character and quirks is what makes them so endearing. What it comes down to, in this miraculous human-to-dog bond, is that every dog has different cognitive skill sets and personality traits that foster a unique connection forever embedded in our lives.

Rhodie loves to stare out the window of her fourteenth-floor home. With the help of a homemade plywood stepstool, she can get to her favorite place, the windowsill.

Megan E. Maxwell, PhD

Certified Applied Animal Behaviorist | PetBehaviorChange.com

I think most people don't realize that a canine behaviorist has had to go through a great deal of education with years of study in many topics that delve into genetics, neurobiology, and physiology, among others, and that they apply rigorous scientific knowledge to canine conduct. You have your PhD and are a certified applied animal behaviorist. What areas of your studies interested you the most?

I was always fascinated by animal behavior and fell in love with behavioral psychology, or behavior analysis, as an undergraduate when I was first introduced to it. The rigorousness and clarity of a scientific approach to understanding behavior has always been very appealing to me. I am perpetually smitten by the fact that learning and behavior follow natural laws and can be examined systematically and objectively. Dog behavior, in particular, was interesting to me because this is a species with whom we humans share such intimacy, historically and presently. The dog plays such an important role in human families and in our emotional landscape. Using science to best understand why dogs do what they do and how they can be best incorporated into our lives while being enriched in theirs was an important goal of mine.

Can you take us through the steps of how dogs learn? Can it ever be just by observation or is it mainly operant conditioning?

Learning by observation, or imitation, has not been widely studied in dogs. Some cases that might appear at first to be imitation may be explained in simpler ways. The overarching types of animal learning are classical conditioning and operant conditioning.

Classical conditioning is often associated with dogs because the famous work of Russian physiologist Ivan Pavlov was conducted with dogs. Pavlov was studying digestion and measuring salivation in dogs when he noticed that dogs who at first would salivate when presented with food (a reflex) soon began to salivate when they saw the experimenter, before food was presented. He then set up various tests to show that, for example, dogs began to salivate to the sound of a bell when this bell was presented just before food. He called this a conditioned reflex, or conditioned response; the dogs had learned that the bell was followed by food and began to salivate upon hearing the bell, a process that required a form of basic learning to occur. In our lives with dogs today, we are observing classical conditioning each time we find our dogs drooling all over us as we prepare their dinner. Of more interest to applied animal behaviorists are those examples of classical conditioning that result in fearful responses to benign events. For example, some dogs will begin to pant, pace, whine, and shake when they hear their owners' keys jingling. In the past, these dogs may have been made anxious by separation from their loved ones when their owner left the home. Over time, the dogs learn that the sound of car keys predicts their owners' departure, and we see the development of a conditioned fearful response to the keys' sound alone. An understanding of classical conditioning can thus play an important role in understanding some of our dogs' basic emotional responses to environmental events.

Operant conditioning is used to characterize a broad spectrum of dog behavior and learning. Many of our dogs' responses are driven by their genetic makeup (species- and breed-specific tendencies), while many others have been learned through the course of the dog's lifetime. These latter responses are products of operant and classical conditioning. Operant conditioning is at work, of course, in dog training (e.g., the use of praise and treats to reward and strengthen desired responses such as sitting, staying, and coming when called), but it is also often at work in the development of canine behavior problems. For example, when a puppy learns that she is often ignored when lying quietly by her owner's side but is petted or talked to each time she whines, she may begin whining more frequently and persistently over time. In this case, we would say that the owner had unintentionally reinforced whining with attention. Our goals in intervention, then, would be to use operant conditioning to turn this around; we would teach the owner to provide attention when her dog was lying quietly by her side and to refrain from providing attention when her dog whined.

What makes some dogs randomly not like each other?
Dogs are more likely to develop fearful or aggressive responses to other dogs when they have not been socialized appropriately with many dogs from a young age. In other cases, dogs can develop fearful or aggressive responses to some other dogs after having been attacked or frightened by a dog. In some cases, a puppy who is attacked by another dog may generalize a fearful response to other dogs of similar size, fur type, or behavior to that of his attacker.

Finally, some dogs are put off by the greeting, interaction, or play style of certain other dogs. A dog might be great meeting dogs who go in for mutual rear-end sniffing but tense at the dogs who sniff her on the face or muzzle. Or, she may be sociable with dogs who can coexist without much interest in her, but becomes defensive with dogs who try to play with her, jump on her back, or chase her. What often appears random to us is far from random from the dog's perspective, and our work as applied animal behaviorists is to help owners better predict and understand those features of other dogs that are making their own dogs uncomfortable.

What's the canine mind processing while engaging in behaviors like humping? I've heard it described as the dog feels insecure.

While we can't delve into the dog's mind directly, we can look to his overt behavior for other signs of anxiety or insecurity. If we see a dog humping in certain situations that are also associated, for example, with panting, furrowed eyebrows, pacing, or other signs of discomfort or ambivalence, then I might be inclined to suspect an insecurity motivation in this case. However, there are other reasons a dog might hump, as well.

Why do dogs constantly observe our faces and seem to be evaluating our emotional state?

Many researchers today are interested in learning more about the social bond between humans and dogs and how this bond influences dog behavior. Part of this bond is emotional (how we feel about our dogs and how we suspect they feel about us), but part of it is also in the ways we communicate across species. This ability for two different species to communicate as well as we do is a truly magnificent feat, taking place over many generations of dogs and humans living and working together. As a species, it is likely that attending to human facial and gestural cues was an adaptive behavioral tendency that evolved over generations. And across the lifespan, dogs learn that the humans in their lives provide them with access to important resources (food, water, exercise, play, and affection) as well as punishment (reprimands, removal from fun situations, etc.), and so looking to our faces and watching our body language are important skills for dogs to have in best predicting upcoming events in their environment.

I've heard a few stories about people being bit unexpectedly by a dog they've just met and how the dog seemed perfectly fine as they were petting them. Can this

happen out of the blue, or do you think there are subtleties of behavioral signs being missed in the moment?

I think it rarely happens "out of the blue." In fact, over fifteen years of practice with hundreds of dogs brought in for behavioral consultations due to aggressive behavior, it is difficult to point out many cases where the aggressive behavior I observed could not have been predicted by the dogs' body language in advance. In the scenario you describe, what most often happens is that people assume that because the dog is standing still and not growling, barking, or snarling, that he or she is enjoying the interaction. In fact, many dogs become still or stiff when they are nervous. If they try to indicate their discomfort by stiffening, and the petting person keeps right on petting the dog, he or she may move to the next line of defense, which may be a snap or a bite.

You have said, "Behavior that produces no positive consequences will not persist while behavior that provides positive reinforcement will be strengthened." Do you think many people struggle with understanding what a proper reaction of consequence to negative behavior is?

Certainly the role of punishment in dog training today is one of the most debated and emotional topics in the field. Over the past several decades, we have seen a paradigm shift in animal training that has paralleled that in parenting and education, away from the use of punishment and toward the increased use of positive reinforcement. This has major benefit for our teachers/trainers and our learners alike. Positive reinforcement has immense potential for teaching all sorts of responses that pet owners might presume their dogs could never learn. At the same time, positive reinforcement has the advantage of being appealing to the animal learner. In fact, we would all prefer to work for positive outcomes than to work only to avoid punishment. By embracing positive reinforcement as the first tool in dog training and rearing, owners are also teaching their dogs to enjoy the learning and training process as a whole.

One great way for owners to think about this when they find themselves angry at their dog for engaging in some problem behavior (chewing shoes, barking at people through the windows, etc.) is to ask themselves what they would like to see instead. That is, instead of chewing shoes, they would like to see their dog chew her own toys. Or, instead of barking at the windows, they would like to see their dog ignore passing people and relax by their feet instead. Then it's just a matter of figuring out how to teach these desirable responses to replace the problematic ones. Working with a qualified pet behavior professional or dog trainer who helps the owner focus on teaching and training in this way can be immensely helpful.

Is it common for mistakes to occur when people anthropomorphize their dogs instead of dealing with it from a canine perspective?

We humans certainly do come at the world from our own perspective—this is unavoidable. In many cases, anthropomorphism is harmless. When anthropomorphism can cause a problem is when we incorrectly attribute an intentionality to our dogs' behavior of which they are not capable and become resentful of our dogs or use it to justify the use of heavy-handed punishment. For example, if an owner observes her dog peeing on her boyfriend's shoes, she may interpret this as jealousy or spite and be resentful of the dog. Or if she finds her dog hiding in the closet when she comes home from work when her dog has peed in the house, she may interpret this as true guilt and feel justified in dragging the dog to the pee spot and reprimanding or swatting him. In both cases, simpler explanations are behind the dogs' behavior and an understanding from the canine perspective should lead to greater empathy for the dog and better solutions to the problem.

What is the most common behavior issue that you are called in to help with? Any easy way to fix that issue?

Ah, if only there was an easy way to address aggression. Aggression is easily the most common behavior problem I am called in to address. It comes in many forms and serves many functions for the dog. The aggression may be directed toward family members or only strangers, toward cats or only small dogs, toward people on walks but only on-leash. Our goal in assessment is to first understand why the aggression is occurring and then develop a function-based intervention that is specific to the client's needs. In every case, we must understand what purpose the aggression serves for the dog so that we can meet that dog's needs in another way while preventing or reducing the aggression.

What's the best way to stop excessive barking?

As with aggression, barking can serve different needs for different dogs. We must first determine why the dog is barking excessively and then develop an individualized behavior plan to address it. Dogs might bark out of boredom, in which case an environmental enrichment plan is developed for the family. Dogs might bark out of fear or defensiveness, in which case we need to assess what aspects of the context are triggering the defensive response and teach the dog to be more comfortable and confident in that context. Some dogs have learned to bark to obtain access to things like walks, attention, or snacks, in which case we need to teach dogs how to obtain these things using calm, quiet behavior instead. There can be no one way to reduce excessive barking without an understanding of why an individual dog is barking excessively in the first place.

What's the oddest issue you've ever seen a dog have that you had to rehabilitate?

I have worked with many dogs exhibiting seemingly mysterious fear responses over the years. I worked with a Bichon who was sent into a panic by the sound of the refrigerator motor kicking on, a Pointer who was petrified of his owner folding laundry, and a Sheltie who hid in the basement every time her owner used the toaster. Recently I even worked with a German Shepherd who was afraid of the sky! For this poor fellow and his owner, walks were frightening and stressful, as the dog ran from one shady spot to the next to avoid open blue skies, constantly scanning his surroundings and ducking for cover.

In all of these cases, we must find a way to develop a systematic desensitization plan that breaks the fear-provoking stimulus or event into manageable steps. We expose the dogs to these steps over time while rewarding calm behavior and ensuring the dog is relaxed at each stage before moving forward.

What's the best way to introduce two dogs for the first time?

This depends on the dogs' history of interactions with other dogs. For dogs who have a history of being friendly and socially appropriate with other dogs, an open space greeting at a park or on a walk can often be all they need for a successful start. If either of the dogs has a history of fear or aggression with other dogs, then a slower introduction might be required. In this case, I often have owners practice walking the dogs at a distance at first while rewarding their own dog's attention to them using the dog's name or "Watch me!" and providing high-value reinforcers such as food or toy access. As the dogs continue to show calm behavior, attending to their owners with no signs of tense focus on each other, I have the owners gradually merge toward each other until they are walking side by side. Walking together can be easier for many dogs than a stationary nose-to-nose greeting because the walk provides distractions for both dogs.

Are your two dogs the most well-behaved, thoroughly understood canines in the country?

I wish I could say so! Instead, you'll often hear me apologizing to my guests when my Plotthound puppy jumps on them and then telling them I need to hire a good dog trainer! However, I do understand why she jumps, and I know exactly what I need to do to address it. Because I am a real person in the real world (raising two preschoolers, working, managing a household, etc.), I am not perfect in implementing all the right strategies all of the time. This realization is helpful to me as I work with families of pets with behavior problems or training deficits; I am reminded to be eternally empathetic to the fact that behavior change is hard. There are rarely any quick fixes; our dogs are always learning whether we intend to be teaching them or not, and we must be persistent, patient, and positive even on our worst days!

Can you share your favorite behavioral story with us?

I have worked with so many wonderful families and so many devoted dog owners over the years that it is hard to pinpoint any one story. There are, however, common themes in many family dynamics that result in conflicts when it comes to the family dog, and successfully resolving some of these conflicts is always deeply gratifying. Many couples face, for example, serious dilemmas when they bring home their first baby and their beloved older dog cannot tolerate this new addition. Other families come to me in tears because their two dogs have begun fighting and they fear that they will have to rehome one of them. I receive many calls from frantic owners whose dog has bitten a neighbor, and they fear they will face a lawsuit or lose their dog because of the incident. In each of these cases, I am thankful to be able to explain to owners that they are not alone and that there are evidence-based and time-tested methods for successfully managing or addressing these situations.

Across all the many scenarios I have been called in to address, I most enjoy watching owners come alive with the understanding of how best to teach and train their dogs and watching dogs come alive with the new clarity provided to them through the effective application of behavior change strategies.

Follow Pet Behavior Change:
Facebook.com/Pet-Behavior-Change
Twitter.com/PBC_LLC

Maddy, 11 years old, English Springer Spaniel, plays *Let's Paint*, App for Dog.

Annie Grossman

Co-owner and Codirector School For The Dogs | SchoolForTheDogs.com

Annie Grossman started out as a journalist, informing the minds of humans. When the financial crisis occurred in 2008, it was the catalyst for her to pursue a dream and switch to enlightening the canine mind as a dog trainer. After completing a certification program with the Karen Pryor Academy of Animal Training and Behavior, she opened the popular School For The Dogs with fellow trainer Kate Senisi. Their center—the only storefront dog training center in New York City—offers private sessions, group sessions, supervised dog play sessions, and many events to expand and enrich a dog's mind. They have helped hundreds of dogs tackle everything from anxiety and aggression to leash skills and skateboard issues.

You say that the training you do at the School For The Dogs is really science-based. Can you expand on that?

The science of behavior is not species specific. Sometimes during a first session, a client will giggle and say something like, "Will this work on my husband?" That's often where I jump in to remind people that humans are animals, too, and the laws of learning apply to us just as much as they apply to dogs, even if some of the ingredients are different. Asking if the science of behavior will work on a human is kind of like asking if gravity will work in Florida.

In the scheme of things, we have way more in common with dogs than we don't. Our common ancestors roamed the earth only 60 million years ago, and, when you consider that there has been life on earth for more than 1 billion years, that's, like, yesterday.

Of course, there are big differences. They don't have thumbs or language; we don't have fur. But we are part of a tiny sliver of life on earth: similarly sized, land-dwelling omnivorous vertebrates not facing extinction. I mean, there's something like 7 million species of animals on earth, and only about 5,500 are mammals! And the majority of the mammals are rodents! All mammals learn in the same way. Nonmammals do, too! But my point is that it's humbling to first find the similarities between us, since we occupy this tiny category together and have evolved to live with each other over the course of more than 10,000 years.

If you can tune in to the fact that you are an animal who is behaving all the time, and you are being affected by the same laws of learning all the time, you'll see you already know a lot more about animal training than you think.

My sessions usually begin with a primer on the two kinds of learning: classical conditioning, which is just a fancy way of saying "learning by association," and operant conditioning, which is learning by consequence. Usually no more than a day or two of high school is devoted to these branches of science, which is crazy to me considering how important they are. Both these kinds of learning are affecting us, and dogs, all the time and are part of the evolutionary process that has helped us both become such successful species. Once you're able to see how these kinds of learning are constantly at play, I think it clears away a lot of the static out there about dog training. There are copious myths about how to train a dog, and most of them are rooted in the idea that some people have a special understanding, or a special power, when it comes to animals. Maybe some people do have some kind of voodoo that makes them able to communicate with dogs in some sort of telepathic way. But it's a relief for people to know that you don't need to have an innate psychic ability to have a happy life with a happy dog.

For the dogs out there who are left home all day—without a walk—waiting for their owners to get home from work, what are the ramifications for the dog fixed in this type of daily routine? What can dog owners do to keep their dogs stimulated and engaged?

I think it's important to consider whether you have a lifestyle that can accommodate a dog. Not everyone does. For those who aren't in a place in their lives where they can't give a dog a happy life, I encourage embracing a larger view of what dog "ownership" is.

A lot of dogs are simply bored. Dog unemployment is a real problem! Dogs evolved to figure things out, solve problems, find things, chase things, kill things and skin them. . . . Today we usually deprive them of those joys by pouring their food into a bowl twice a day. Training can be a great way to keep your dog's brain working in ways that will keep him happy and net good manners. Even if you're just teaching silly stuff, it's still a good dog-brain workout.

There are also lots of more passive things you can do that can help a dog be occupied. Sometimes that means just encouraging someone to find a neighbor who works from home who maybe has a dog your dog can play with during the day. More often than not, the easiest way to engage their "seeking" need is to put their food in toys that make them have to "work" for their food. In my house, pretty much everything is a food toy before it goes in the recycling bin—putting kibble in an empty water bottle that can be kicked around is an easy one. But there are an increasing number of great toys on the market that help burn a dog's time and energy and require little more human effort than pouring food into a bowl would. If we don't give dogs jobs, they will make up their own jobs, and you probably weren't looking to hire someone to redesign the legs of your coffee table with their teeth.

You've received a great deal of press on using iPads with your dog students for target training. If my dog attends a class, will he be taking selfies at the end of the day or creating some beautiful drawings?

Touchscreen devices can be great for people who are just starting to learn how to train a dog because they provide immediate feedback. We teach "targeting" to every dog who comes in the door—targeting is simply touching one body part to something. We often start with a nose-to-hand touch, because it's easy for a dog to learn and is a building block toward lots of other behaviors. Essentially, everything breaks down to some kind of targeting—sitting is butt-to-ground targeting; "look" is eyes-to-eyes targeting. A handheld clicker is something we show people how to use to help communicate to a dog the exact moment he does something correctly; it is followed by a treat, but for many reasons, it's usually more effective to use the clicker in training rather than trying to get a treat into a dog's mouth the moment he does the correct thing.

Sometimes, instead of doing nose-to-hand touch, I'll have a client basically teach nose-to-iPhone-in-my-hand touch. I use an app that makes a "ding" and a mark on the screen the moment the dogs touches the iPhone. It's usually not hard to get them to touch it if you hold it close to their faces, because they're used to exploring the world with their noses. Sometimes a tiny smear of peanut butter can help get the ball rolling at first (you can put your phone in a plastic baggie or put plastic wrap on the screen if you fear it getting slobbered upon). By using the iPhone ding to indicate the moment of the touch, rather than clicking the moment of the touch, a new trainer can get some nice precision without a lot of coordination required. And you'll get a little drawing out of it, as well!

Do you have any favorite toys that you find are best for mental stimulation?

There are three categories of toys: 1) Toys that they bat around and stuff comes out, which are best used with treats or dry food; 2) "Slow food" bowls, or what I call "bowls with stuff going on in them." These can be used for wet or dry food, and the dog essentially has to eat around little obstacles that are in the bowl; and 3) Puzzle toys, which usually have drawers that have to be opened, or pegs pulled out, to get to the food. These are sometimes for dogs who are a bit more advanced and may contain small pieces that aren't suitable for a puppy. But there are some really cool puzzle toys out there. I particularly like the ones made by the Swedish company Nina Ottosson. *(For more on Nina Ottosson, go to her interview on page 170.)*

I cringe when I hear about shock collars or growling back at your dog or needing to dominate your dog for him/her to listen to you. School For The Dogs is based on positive reinforcement. From the cognitive perspective of how a dog is wired, why is this approach so much more effective?

There are a lot of reasons I don't advocate using aversive techniques with dogs, but the big one—and I think the one that's simplest to understand—is that dogs often make the wrong associations with things. So he runs through an electric fence and gets a shock, but he might not necessarily know that it was crossing a boundary that earned him the zing. He might think it was looking at the UPS man who just pulled up. Now you have a dog who thinks UPS men cause shocks, and that is going to lead to a whole other set of problems. I think punishment can have similar collateral damage when used on humans, but at least language lets us explain to someone why we are punishing them. Another problem is that it can generalize really quickly. John Watson, the early-twentieth-century psychologist who is considered one of the founders of behaviorism, did a famous experiment where he showed a baby with a bunch of objects and animals (a dog, a monkey, a rabbit, a newspaper, some yarn, etc). The baby had no major reaction to any of them. Then he brought back the rabbit and made a huge clanging noise behind the baby's back. The next time the baby saw the rabbit, he was terrified. But he also was then fearful of all the other things to which he had previously had little reaction. Unfortunately, I think that experiment is played out in real life with dogs all the time.

Your co-owner, Kate Senisi, is known for her "holistic approach with an emphasis on creativity" in dealing with offering solutions for behavioral-challenged dogs. Can you give an example of how she does this?

Kate and I make a great team for many reasons, one of which is that she really likes working with what we call "reactive" dogs—dogs who have, let's say, issues. I generally prefer working with puppies, where I can kind of help someone start off on the right foot so they don't end up having a dog who needs to see Kate!

Another example is that I'm someone who is good at thinking on her feet and helping people see big-picture stuff, where Kate excels at creating detailed-but-easy-to-follow longitudinal plans and breaking things down in such a way that someone only has to deal with the moment they're in, rather than being overwhelmed by the larger problem. By helping find solutions that fit into people's lives, and by focusing on setting up both the dog and the human client for success, she is able to help people solve their issues—but what's more amazing than that is that they often want to keep coming back to us even when they've attained their goals! She is able to take stressful situations and turn them into training experiences that are just that much fun.

You offer "Breed Meet-Ups" at your center, which I find fascinating! It's an opportunity for dogs of the same breed and their loved ones to get together and socialize. You even serve coffee or wine. If you had to generalize a few of the breeds' behaviors, can you share some of your observations?

Our breed meet-ups are really just an excuse to attract people who might not otherwise come to the kind of safe, controlled dog/human gatherings we host. It's a way to get people in the door—we don't actually discriminate at our breed meet-ups, and it isn't uncommon to come in and see, like, four Wheaten terriers, and then a Schnauzer and a Yorkie. I don't generally see breeds in terms of like-characteristics, because individuals are each just so different. I think more in terms of personality types, and I think at least some of that stuff is baked in and can be passed down, perhaps in certain lines of certain breeds. Just like with people, some people are kind of quiet and thoughtful from birth, while others are more out there. There is a stereotype of Golden Retrievers being happy-go-lucky, and while I've seen some who are not like that at all, I definitely have seen some who seem to take everything lightly and are just friendly and goofy and easily pleased.

You see a lot of dogs come in and out of your center. Can you share a couple of your favorite stories?

What comes to mind is all the happy street encounters I have with my students. Sometimes I'll run into one on the street, with their owner or a walker, and the greeting I get is unreal. It's such a joy to watch them suddenly recognize me and then get excited. And then I'm always sort of touched when I walk away and see them not budging, trying to get their person to go in the direction I'm going in.

It's also sweet that we have a lot of dogs who play what I call "reverse hooky," where they pull their owners to School For The Dogs even if we are closed, or if we are doing a private session. Sometimes I'll be in the middle of a lesson, and out of the corner of my eye, I'll see one of our regulars on the other side of the glass door, sitting patiently. They know that we require a sit before we open the door, and they are sitting with all they've got.

Follow School For The Dogs
Facebook.com/schoolforthedogs
Instagram.com/schoolforthedogs

Evan MacLean

Assistant Professor, School of Anthropology, University of Arizona | Director, Arizona Canine Cognition Center | Dogs.Arizona.edu

You have extensively studied the relationship between humans and dogs and have presented hard facts about the benefits of bringing your dog to work. More and more companies are getting onboard with this concept. Can you explain how dogs can help employees relieve stress, enhance creativity, and boost productivity? Having dogs in a work environment can bring about a lot of good things, but there can be some challenges inherent to this, as well. A lot of the benefits we get from dogs relate to their ability to help us de-stress and to provide a bridge for social interactions. There are dozens of studies now illustrating that calm interactions with dogs can yield beneficial biological effects, including a reduction in cortisol levels (a

key player in the body's stress response), lower heart rate and blood pressure, and an increase in oxytocin—a neurohormone involved in promoting calm states and social engagement. Too much stress can actually interfere with cognition and get in the way of getting things done effectively. So these stress-reducing benefits have great potential to help keep us sharp and composed at work.

Dogs can often bring us together socially, as well. There are some great studies that show people are much more likely to be talked to, or approached by others, when they are with a dog. This may seem like a small thing, but if somebody stops to say hello in a situation where they otherwise wouldn't, this can help keep workers engaged with one another, exchanging ideas, and cultivating a sense of togetherness. In today's hectic work environments, it's easy to blitz past one another, and sometimes dogs help us find an extra moment to slow down and connect with those around us.

Although there are a lot of potential benefits of having dogs at work, this is something that needs to be thought through carefully and dealt with on a case-by-case basis. For example, some people have allergies, dogs may be distracting, or somebody who was recently bitten by a dog may be anxious or fearful around animals at work. So thoughtful and conscientious implementation is important.

There is a tremendous amount of diversity within the dog species. When you are researching genetic traits in connection to behavior, are you finding any categorical breed-centric characteristics that are rather universal?

Although there are strong stereotypes about breed-specific behavior, we tend to find a lot of variation within all of the breeds we have studied. So while on average Labradors may be more enthused to play fetch than Pomeranians, there will be plenty of exceptions to this rule. Genetic factors certainly contribute to behavioral differences between breeds, but these distinctions are rarely categorical in nature. The study of breed differences in cognition is really in its infancy, but this is an area where we are very excited about potential for future discoveries.

One of the things that has many scientists excited about dogs is that they are one of the most diverse species on the planet. Within the same species, we have breeds that can literally fit inside teacup, and those that can weigh upwards of two hundred pounds. And size is just one example of incredible diversity within dogs—we see similar variance across a whole range of traits. Do we see similar diversity in terms of how different breeds think? We don't have confident answers to this question yet, but it's a very active area of inquiry.

What do you think is going on in the dog's mind when he or she is just staring at their owner? They seem to be studying our communicative gestures and reading our mood, and even engaging in emotional contagion. Why do they have a need to do this?

A lot of people wonder what's going on in a dog's head during these moments. The truth is that there are lots of reasons why dogs may engage in this behavior. Any dog owner can tell you that dogs pick up on the subtlest of cues when it comes to things like when they will get a walk, playtime, or their dinner. So, dogs are often looking to humans as a telltale of what's about to happen next—and hopefully that's dinner! But other times, a dog's gaze may simply be a form of affection. In many species, directly staring at another individual is a threat and not something to take lightly, but in the context of close relationships, eye gaze can take on other meanings, as it does in intimate human relationships. There have been several studies now that specifically link gaze between humans and dogs to increases in oxytocin in both individuals, and it's likely that this hormone contributes to the positive feelings we have toward each other. So as your pup relaxes and stares at you, it's quite possible she's enjoying an intoxicating release of neurochemicals.

A recent study came out saying that dogs don't like to be hugged. Dog owners were collectively infuriated and criticized these findings by offering their own anecdotal evidence stating otherwise. What is your stance on this hot topic?
It's important to note that this was a bit of an informal experiment, and not one designed to rigorously test this question, but what's important to realize here is that hugging is not really in the dog's natural repertoire of affiliative behaviors. Humans, and other primates, take a lot of comfort from a hug, and so it feels natural to do this with our pets, but hugging can essentially immobilize an animal and has a lot of potential to make them feel trapped or anxious. This is not to say that dogs don't like physical affection—they certainly do! But there are other ways to cuddle with your pup without wrapping them up in a big bear hug. The kind of affection a dog prefers can vary a lot from individual to individual, so the best advice to is pay close attention to how the dog responds to different kinds of contact and to see what they seem to enjoy most.

Out of all your years of canine research, what is the most surprising finding you have discovered?
A lot people like to ask questions like "Which breed is the smartest?" or "Are dogs smarter than cats?" One of the most important things we have discovered is that

these are really the wrong questions to be asking. What we've learned is that there are multiple different dimensions to animal minds, just as there are in humans. One individual might be great at solving memory problems, but very limited in what they can pick up in a social setting, whereas another animal may show the opposite pattern. Neither one is "smarter" than the other; they just have different profiles of strengths and weaknesses. It's easy to wrap our minds around this when we think about humans. For example, we recognize that the cognitive skills that make somebody a great engineer might be different from what makes someone an insightful therapist or a political mastermind. These are different cognitive skill sets, and animal cognition comes in many varieties, as well. We see this both within and between species. Dogs are an interesting example of this in that they are remarkably sophisticated when solving some problems, particularly those with a social component, but can be clueless in other contexts. So, don't ask, "How smart is a dog?" but rather, "How is a dog smart?"

Rosie enjoys finding treats with the Dog Fighter™ game.

Nina Ottosson

Globally Acclaimed Designer of Interactive Dog Puzzles | Nina-Ottosson.com

Nina Ottosson is a highly respected inventor of intelligent puzzle games and toys for dogs. She has created a whole new category of toys that provide fun and appealing ways to stimulate a dog's brain while challenging their dexterity and reinforcing their relationship with people. Nina has been heralded in *Dog Fancy* as one of the People Who Have Changed the Dog World, and she continues to design and produce unique, award-winning products that not only genuinely engage dogs, but also enable them to problem-solve.

You started this business, essentially because of a bad conscience! After having two children a year apart, it was difficult to have the time to mentally stimulate your dogs as you once did. What was the first toy you designed?

I started around 1990, and my first inventions were the Qulan treat ball, where the dog has to roll out treats, and the DogSmart in wood, where the dog has to lift up blocks to reveal hidden treats.

Most dog owners know the importance of physical stimulation, but why is mental activity so important, too?

That is the key to a healthy, happy dog, and the only way to really get a dog to be tired, using the brain with problem-solving in different ways. Some dogs need it more than others.

I am very proud that I created the category of mental puzzle games and toys worldwide, and that people have realized the important connection between mental stimulation (or lack thereof) and behavior problems.

My mission has always been to get the message out to as many people as possible about the importance of mental stimulation. Dogs have four legs and one brain, and all five need to be activated. Many so-called "problem dogs" are actually just bored. If we give all dogs both mental and physical stimulation each day, the number of problem dogs will be substantially reduced.

Dogs as well as cats really need to use their brain, and they don't get to do enough of that today. Their natural instinct is to hunt for food, but we mostly serve them their food in a bowl instead for letting them work for it in different ways. So many indoor cats and dogs are bored. They will be so much happier and healthier if they get to use their brains. It can help prevent a lot of behavioral problems such as chewing, barking, hyperactivity, obesity, and more.

Can you explain why your puzzles and games are so crucial to injured or older dogs?

For injured or convalescent dogs, it's very important for their overall health to keep them mentally active without moving around, especially for high-energy dogs who can be very difficult to calm down. Puzzle-solving keeps them mentally busy without moving around, and if the dog is in pain, it's sometimes the only way to get him to eat. The same for older dogs—their bodies don't have the same capacity to move around as they did when they were younger, but their brains are still very active, and puzzle-solving is fun and keeps the brain alert. It's the same for us humans—if we use our brains for problem-solving daily, it reduces the risk of depression and Alzheimer's disease.

You are an expert in knowing what games and puzzles dogs like, but have you created any products that have become an unexpected hit?

I test my ideas and products carefully with a lot of different dogs before I launch them, so I know the dogs will like them. I create puzzles in different sizes, materials, and difficulty levels, because all dogs have different sizes, mental capacities, and skills, so all puzzles might not suit all dogs, but several of them will suit just your dog.

How are you able to design so many new, fun, and engaging toys and puzzles? What inspires you?

I love to design puzzles and other pet-related products. I have a lot of ideas all the time, and the fun part is figuring out ideas together with my dogs. I am inspired from my own dogs and all my customers and friends around the world, who thank me for changing their dogs' lives and also their own lives. I know I also have inspired other pet owners and zoos to start with puzzle-solving and animal enrichment, and what an enormous difference it makes to let the animal work for their food instead of serving it in a bowl.

What is the best way to increase the challenging aspects of a puzzle once the dog understands how it works? Can all of your creations get increasingly harder for the dog to master? Your toys and puzzle games are rated on a level of one to three. Can you explain that system?

Dogs have different levels of intelligence just like us humans. I realized from the beginning that my puzzle games must have different levels of difficulty to fit as many dogs as possible. In addition, some dogs with a genetic disposition for fetching will find certain games easier than dogs that first have to learn how to fetch. All dogs enjoy a variety of activities and appreciate trying new things. The same goes for these games—some dogs are happy with games that are simple and easy, while others need increasingly difficult ones. It's the same for us humans and crossword puzzles—some people are happy with the simple ones, while others continue to challenge themselves with ones that are more and more difficult. Some of my puzzles can be varied both a little harder and easier by adding or removing pegs and blocks.

A tip to make the puzzle harder is to put the game on a chair or stool, so that the dog can only work with the nose, which can be much more difficult than working with the paws. This is excellent also when the dog is injured and not able to move around.

A tip for energetic dogs with the plastic puzzles, for example the DogTwister and the DogTornado, is to make a meaty ice cream for your dog by mixing some meaty dog food with water and pouring some of the mixture in the hollows (you could also place a small piece of sausage or a little tasty treat in each hollow and pour in a little water), put the game in the freezer, and let it set. This is perfect for very active dogs when it's hot, or when the dog needs some extra activity. As always with treat toys/puzzles, use it under supervision.

You have described one of your own dogs as "not the most intelligent," but you love his energy. Is it possible to increase a dog's aptitude by stimulating his mind on a regular basis?

Yes, it's absolutely possible by regularly challenging the dog's mind by teaching, praising, and encouraging every step forward. It's also very important to use the reward your dog appreciates most of all.

Have you ever encountered a dog who didn't want to bother with a game or puzzle?

About 20 to 25 percent of all dogs are not really motivated to be rewarded by food or treats, but some of them I have succeeded in getting them excited enough to solve a puzzle if it's filled with "frozen meaty ice cream" (see above).

Why do you recommend fifteen to twenty minutes' rest after puzzle time?

With all kinds of dog training, body or brain, it's important to rest, recover, and calm down between each session, especially with younger dogs and energetic dogs. The dog can be stressed if each session of training is too long; it's difficult to keep concentration and learn new things for a longer time, and the dog can end up frustrated, which is not positive. It's just as important to find a balance of activity and inactivity, so that the dog does not get stressed by under- or overactivity.

Can you share your favorite dog story that involves one of your puzzles?

Several years ago, a friend got a rescue dog, a Cocker Spaniel. She was about three years old, overweight, and understimulated. At first she did not seem very intelligent, and she was very shy. When we began testing the easiest games, she acted like she did not want to play or dare to understand how to act. She didn't even want to look at the puzzle. She simply didn't want to try because she had never played with a human before, never been encouraged to be curious and playful and explore the world from when she was a puppy. After a certain amount of time, we saw that she started understanding what to do and started trying more and more. Her self-confidence was growing, and she really showed pure happiness with her tail wagging when she was successful and started finding the treats. With lots of praise and with increased self-confidence and trust, she began solving all my difficult puzzles. She later became a model for some of my puzzles.

Last, can you share some little-known fun facts about your toys and puzzles?
My puzzles are used with therapy dogs in hospitals. Also, other pets can use them, too: cats, minipigs, parrots, ferrets, lizards, wildcats, monkeys, etc.

Follow Nina Ottosson
Instagram.com/nina_ottosson
Facebook.com/ninaottossonpuzzles
Twitter.com/nina_ottosson

Body

INSIDE THE CANINE WELLNESS AND HEALTH, THE EXPERT INTERVIEWS

The Body section represents the physical facets of a dog, from breed, size, agility, and exercise to internal aspects of nutrition, health, and wellness management. Beginning with nutrition, more and more dog owners are educating themselves, reading labels, avoiding food filled with grains, and not buying treats or food made in China. Comparable to the global shift that began for humans nearly two decades ago in choosing organic, and buying more produce from farmers' markets, the pet food industry soon caught up and followed suit. The newfound heightened awareness created by major pet food recalls in 2007 and 2012 revealed that even many United States-based kibble companies were using a premix from China that contained melamine, which was responsible for more than one hundred pet deaths and more than five hundred cases of kidney failure.[7] Since then, many pet owners have chosen to forgo processed dog foods and instead feed either raw or home-prepared meals. Clare Kearney, a holistic canine nutritionist from Australia, explains in this section that "holistic nutrition is basically just eating fresh, whole foods from nature" as she guides us through the process of making a balanced and healthy diet from our own kitchens. Speaking of food in the kitchen, we learned how motivating that can be for dogs like Buddy, Harley, Rosie, and Monty, who, when unattended for just a minute, will go to extremes to climb counters, chairs, and tables to devour whatever grub they can find!

Holistic pet care industry leaders Randi and Phil Klein, owners of Whiskers Holistic Pet Care in New York City, have made healthy pet food and supplement education their life's work. Their store offers a free, open consultation area where

---

7   *Associated Press* (28 March 2007). "104 Deaths Reported in Pet Food Recall." *New York Times*. Retrieved 2007–04–11.

they spend time answering a variety of customer questions about all types of dog conditions. Holistic veterinarian Dr. Marty Goldstein discusses revealing insights of the root cause of many of these common conditions, and Dr. Jill Elliot offers homeopathic remedies to treat some of the most common problems. Chief medical officer of the Veterinarian Cancer Center, Dr. Gerald Post, discusses cancer, which has become the most common canine illness today, and offers hope for the future.

Our furry friends often demonstrate acts of physicality that impress, such as Sunny's dexterity in skillfully opening doors and Buster's ability to open the refrigerator, throw items in the garbage, and take clothes out of the dryer. There's also three-legged Cooper, who impresses just by nimbly getting around. Dr. Gene Giggleman explains canine chiropractic care and how to keep their dynamic, muscular, and skeletal systems in alignment, and Kim Freeman gives helpful tips you can do yourself for massage, which dogs like Sedona look forward to. Although some dogs, like the athletic Lou Lou, enjoy a different kind of massage—getting dragged on the grass by her leash—much to the shock of appalled bystanders.

A dog's breed, age, and size determine the intensity and type of activity that best suit him, and it's a good idea to speak to your veterinarian when starting a new regimen. A regular schedule of exercise—not just indolently sticking your dog in the yard—is an utter necessity in obtaining optimal physical (and mental) wellness that all the dogs featured in this book engage in. Water activity, in its many forms from therapeutic to rigorous, is essential to dogs like Jock, who receives hydrotherapy; Baci and Pesto, who spend hours in the pool; and Clay, who swims at the beach and runs alongside a bike every day. Tate participates in a daily, varied level of activity that's both extraordinary and exhausting to list. On the other hand, the simple, regular walks are of such great value, too, as dog walker Laura Turley reminds us. It enables opportunities for connection with the community, like how Dora so valuably does for her elderly companion. Dogs experience the world in a much more physical way, through smell and movement, and their experiences, like those of humans, profoundly affect them. Moments of connectivity and increased activity levels are two of the ancillary, physical benefits that dogs provide to their loved ones.

Our experts concur that some easy changes you can implement to enhance your dog's well-being are to read food labels, don't overvaccinate, research the new vaccination data, and integrate alternative therapies when needed. Most important, make sure you get out in nature with your dog and enjoy a hike together, because nothing promotes the dog-human bond more than a shared physical activity.

Clare Kearney

Holistic Canine Nutritionist | HUNDE.com.au

You have said, "I am really, acutely aware that 'holistic canine nutrition' as an industry sounds like a load of wank" and that you understand how people associate "holistic with the trendy buzz words and think that it's an elitist practice of dog care." Can you explain what you mean by *holistic canine nutrition* and why at first people might roll their eyes at this term?

I think we have overcomplicated nutrition and now there is this chasm between people who choose to eat highly processed foods, either for their enjoyment or because they don't know any better, and those who seemingly consume (and Instagram) exclusively exotic, organic wonder foods. I regularly roll my eyes at that! It's unnecessary, and it makes eating well seem overwhelming. For me, holistic nutrition as a whole (both for humans and dogs—my philosophy is the same for each) is the middle ground between the two. Fresh, species-appropriate foods. For dogs, this is primarily meat and bones. Not that complicated or elitist!

I also think a part of the eye-roll factor may come from equating or confusing

holistic nutrition with holistic or alternative medicine. I am personally a big fan of holistic medicine, but I understand there is a lot of rhetoric surrounding some practices (such as homeopathy) being pseudoscience and/or a waste of money. It's not my place to say either way on that matter, but I think holistic nutrition is a lot less controversial and a lot simpler in the sense that it is basically just about eating fresh, whole foods from nature. This way, the animal is receiving a steady stream of the nutrients that it requires to build a healthy immune system, which is the number-one defense against illness. Getting people to understand that holistic nutrition, especially when it comes to dogs, isn't some junk science designed to relieve people of their hard-earned cash is a big part of the battle. But for me, it doesn't make any sense to treat a symptom without first looking for a cause, which we so often do in the case of our pets.

You say that a dog's digestive system is primarily designed to eat raw meat. Can you explain why?

Dogs have the teeth, jaws, and digestive system of a carnivore. Beginning in the mouth, their teeth are sharp and pointed, specifically designed to rip and tear flesh. Their jaws are hinged to open widely and swallow large chunks, and they only move vertically, not side to side. This combination of a vertically moving jaw and no flat molars make grinding plant matter very difficult. Tellingly, dogs also do not produce salivary amylase, which is the enzyme herbivores and omnivores produce in their saliva to begin the digestion of starches before they reach the stomach. They simply don't need it.

Dogs' stomachs are highly acidic, and they hold food in their stomachs for up to eight hours, which facilitates the digestion of meat, bones, and fat, while creating an inhospitable environment for bacteria. This is the reason dogs can tolerate eating rancid meat without becoming unwell. Once food leaves the stomach, small amounts of food quickly pass through the dog's intestines, which are very short (around two feet). Comparatively, humans (who are omnivores) hold food in their stomachs for around an hour, before passing it to the intestines, where it may remain for days and is consequently much more susceptible to bacteria.

Because of this digestive makeup, feeding large amounts of plant matter to dogs will result in it sitting in the stomach all day and then quickly passing through the brief GI tract, which doesn't have the required capacity to break down plant cellulose. This can cause digestive stress, gas, and excessive waste.

Why is a raw diet so controversial? For every vet who recommends it, there is one who doesn't. Why is that?

I think in part it's just that it's not the status quo. For the past hundred years, we've fed dogs primarily processed dog foods, and now people are turning around and saying we shouldn't do that; it can take some getting used to.

I make a really concerted effort to emphasize the important distinction between dogs and humans when it comes to nutrition—my overall philosophy regarding holistic nutrition is the same for both, but the practical application is very different—and I think this is extremely relevant when it comes to the idea of feeding raw meat. We are taught that raw meat will make you sick, and we instinctively know that eating it is pretty disgusting. But dogs are different. Their digestive systems are specifically designed for it, and they love it!

In terms of why the veterinary industry is so divided, that's a little more complex, but fortunately I think it is shifting. I'm not a vet and I didn't go to veterinary school, so I can only base my views on the research I have done, but my understanding is that the veterinary industry and the pet food industry have a long and intertwined history. I believe nutrition was also not widely taught in veterinary courses for a very long time, so I imagine a simple lack of education must play a role.

That said, an unbalanced raw diet can be just as bad for a dog as a processed diet, so I highly recommend finding and speaking to a vet or a nutritionist who advocates feeding raw before attempting to prepare your dog's food yourself.

How can kibble and canned food lead to fat, itchy, smelly dogs?

Where do I start? Perhaps at the beginning, where the problems start. Unlike a natural diet that includes bones, these foods do not clean dogs' teeth, so a dog fed exclusively kibble or canned food is likely to quickly develop periodontal issues, which can lead to a life of pain. The buildup of food on teeth can also cause bacteria to enter the body, leading to internal inflammation and a host of subsequent health issues. Not to mention seriously bad doggy breath.

Feeding a lot of grains and plant matter, which most processed pet foods are very high in, can cause dogs to gain weight, as they need to eat a lot more to meet their nutritional requirements. As I've mentioned, their digestive system is also not equipped to digest grains and starches, so they do not process or extract nutrients from these foods efficiently. Large quantities of grains will also likely lead to large, smelly stools, as the plant matter they cannot digest is expelled as waste.

When it comes to skin conditions in dogs, yeast is a key issue. Yeast is present naturally in dogs, but an overgrowth is a common cause of serious itchiness. Canned foods and kibble tend to be high in starch (even grain-free varieties!), which turns to sugar and feeds yeast, leading to overgrowths and sometimes very severe and unpleasant skin conditions.

Repeated exposure to allergens is also commonplace when feeding the same kibble or canned food over extended periods of time—sometimes even the dog's entire lifetime! This repeated exposure could trigger an overactive immune response, also known as an allergic reaction, when the body no longer recognizes the allergen as food. This may present as digestive upset, skin conditions, or both.

Ultimately, the reason these foods can cause health problems in dogs is that they do not supply the fresh nutrients required to support a strong immune system. A dog with a compromised immune system is more susceptible to many illnesses. Much of the immune system resides within the gut, so nutrition is crucial to its health. I would add that a dog might be more susceptible to seasonal allergies if their immune system is already under stress from a poor diet.

What do you think would happen to the dog that only ate a plant-based diet?
I couldn't say for certain what would happen, but I know it is not the best diet for a healthy dog, so it's one I would never endorse. Dogs have difficulty digesting and extracting the nutrients, particularly protein, from plant-based sources. As I mentioned earlier, their digestive system is simply not designed for it. Plant-based sources also do not contain all of the amino acids dogs require. Dogs' nutrient requirements are different from those of human beings, so for them to meet their nutritional needs from a plant-based diet (if this is even possible, which I'm not convinced it is), they

would need to consume a significantly larger amount of food. Consuming such large amounts of food, especially grains, can result in serious digestive distress, as well as a much greater risk of obesity—and with it all of the associated health problems. This food would also need to be heavily fortified with synthetic nutrients.

Basically a plant-based diet comes with all of the downsides of heavily processed dog food, with the added bonus of not containing the main food group (meat) dogs require for optimum health. Ultimately, I think what would happen is they would likely be in a fairly constant state of digestive distress, they may experience skin conditions due to a yeast overgrowth, they would probably experience periodontal issues in the long term, they may become overweight from excess plant matter, and they would struggle to meet their nutritional needs, which could lead to a whole host of issues.

What is the best way to transition a dog into a raw diet if they've never eaten raw?
This is something that will vary from dog to dog. Many dogs have an iron stomach and will take to it like a fish to water with little or no negative effect. Others may require a little more finesse, and some will take serious convincing.

As a general guide, I would recommend fasting your dog (although not puppies) for a day to make sure they're not still digesting their old food, as adding new food to this may cause digestive stress. Skipping the morning or evening meal should be sufficient.

Then I would start with something simple like a meal of chicken—breast or thighs if you want to ease into bones, or a wing or some necks can be added if you're feeling brave. Bones may actually help the transition because they firm up stools. If this is well tolerated, I'd give it a few days or a week and then introduce a second protein. Beef, lamb, turkey, rabbit, fish. . . From here, all of these (and more) can be introduced gradually and monitored to check for any adverse reactions.

If your dog isn't sure what to do with the bones, you may need to make some cuts in the meat to help them work it out, or sometimes holding the bone for them will help.

Organ meat is one thing that sometimes poses a challenge. Some dogs just don't seem to like it, and others struggle with the texture. However, it's an important addition to the diet, so you need to make sure they're getting some. Definitely wait until they have completely settled into eating raw before you attempt to add organ meat, and I would recommend feeding it with a particularly bony meal (something like chicken frames), as it can cause loose stools. If your dog isn't so keen, it may help to dice it into small pieces, or you might have to make a bit of an organ mixture in the blender or food processor. Eventually, they should just get used to it. Another trick is to give a reluctant dog their organ meat first (while they're hungry) and withhold the rest of the meal until they've eaten it.

What proteins are highest in allergy potential? Which ones are the least?
This really depends on the dog. To the best of my knowledge, there is nothing inherent to any one protein that makes it more of an allergen than others. Some dogs present an adverse reaction to cooked chicken but not raw—there are no rules. A great way to avoid allergy reactions is to ensure the diet is varied. Repeated exposure to potential allergens may trigger an overactive immune response (i.e., an allergy), so feeding a single protein is more likely to induce such a reaction than if you're feeding a variety or switching proteins regularly.

You've written about the importance of giving a dog a raw bone. Should you be careful about splintering? What kind of bone is best?
The best bone is something that, to an extent, will also depend on the dog, and more specifically on its size. There are two kinds of bones you can feed: meaty bones and recreational bones. Meaty bones are things like chicken wings (a great choice for most dogs), which is whole with meat still attached and which the dog will consume completely. This would form a part of the dog's regular food, and I highly recommend feeding meaty bones, since they naturally offer a well-balanced source of nutrients. Recreational bones are generally larger bones, like marrowbones that the dog will chew on and tear the meat from but not fully

consume. In reality, larger bones are actually safer because the dog will need to chew it before swallowing.

Splintering is not a major issue, so long as bones are fed raw, which they *always* should be. Cooked bones do pose a significant risk of splintering and should never be fed. Some bones are also considered too hard and risk damaging teeth, such as weight-bearing bones from large animals. The most important thing when feeding bones to your dog is to get to know it and watch it. Once you feel confident with what they can handle, I say go for it! Bones provide a necessary source of calcium, clean teeth, and also offer important mental stimulation.

Top Tips to Transform Canine Health

- Give your dog a raw bone for dental health and mental stimulation.
- Go grain/starch-free to reduce skin irritation and digestive upset.
- Feed a variety of proteins, including oily fish and organ meat, for a steady supply of fresh, natural nutrients and a healthy, happy dog.

Feeding your dog healthfully can be expensive. Do you have any tips on how to do it on a budget?

Get to know your local butcher or fresh food market. You'd be amazed by what they keep under the counter! Often you can get cuts of meat that are not popular with people for very cheap—hearts, chicken frames, fish heads, offal—and all of this is incredibly nutritious stuff. Dogs don't need to eat prime cuts. Buying in bulk can reduce costs, and always keep an eye out for specials. I find my supermarket often marks down their offal when it gets close to out of date.

Keep it simple. You don't need to give a healthy dog expensive supplements. A balanced, varied raw diet will supply the nutrients a dog requires for a healthy immune system and largely reduce the need for supplementation.

The other thing to remember is that feeding your dog a raw, natural diet will often cost less than high-end commercial dog food, and in the long term you will be saving money on things like vet bills.

What do you hope to see in the future for the trajectory of holistic nutrition?
I'm excited to see holistic nutrition becoming more and more popular, with both humans and their canine (and feline) companions adapting to more natural ways of eating. I hope that this will continue and eventually we will get back to most dogs eating a species-appropriate diet and processed dog food, as we know it no longer is the norm. Ultimately, this will result in happier, healthier, longer-living dogs, which is the most I can possibly hope for!

Follow HUNDE
Facebook: facebook.com/hunde.au
Twitter: @HUNDE_au
Instagram: @Hunde.au

IN LOVING MEMORY
TEDI-ANNE — 1990-2006
CAMI-ANNE — 1985-2011
RACHEL-ANNE - 1983-2011
MAGGIE-MAE - 1983-2012
XENA-MARIE-1997-2015

Randy Klein

Co-owner, Whiskers Holistic Pet Care | 1800whiskers.com

Randi and Phil Klein are the owners of Whiskers Holistic Pet Care in New York City. They've been in business for thirty years and are known as pioneers in holistic pet care. A decade ago, they hosted the first-ever Natural Pet Care Expo with the intention of educating and enlightening pet owners with speakers, exhibitors, and workshops. Education and advice is their life's work, offering carefully vetted products, food, toys, and supplements, as well as their open consultation area where pet owners can get free advice for any type of pet malady.

You began when it wasn't popular and when most people equated the term *holistic pet care* to wacky new-agey practices. Now, not only is the natural pet

care industry booming, but holistic food and grooming products have become the number-one choice for millions of pet owners garnering sales in the *300 billions* last year! What was the motivation to start this business, and why was this important to you? What have you learned along the way?

You're right. When we began, people thought we were wacky, crazy, "out there." The concept of a more natural diet for their pets was something people just did not think about. When the great recall of several years ago happened, and people's pets were literally dying, something changed—big-time. It was okay to start reading labels and checking food sources. We started because of a personal situation with our beloved Tiffany-Anne. Thirteen at the time, she developed bone cancer. After using allopathic medicine (and it was not successful), we found ourselves down a path we had never even heard of. We, too, like our customers to come, thought, "Wow, this is crazy." But a whole new world opened up to us, and we haven't looked back since.

What does the term *holistic* mean to you in terms of pet care?

Holistic means, in the easiest way to understand, "looking at an entire picture of an ailment, disease, or condition." Kind of like the old rhyme, the knee bone is connected to the shinbone, the shinbone is connected to the thighbone, and so on. You must look at all the parts to see the real problem.

I love your open consultation area in the back. Customers can count on Phil for his experienced, tell-it-like-it-is advice. Whiskers has a reputation as a place where customers can come in and share their pet concerns and your staff is super knowledgeable, they listen intently, and they ask a lot of questions to make sure that they are recommending the right product. To what do you attribute this?

Phil and I have always felt treating people the way we want to be treated goes without much saying. We instill in our staff our passion for helping the animals. When we started, there were no places or people we could turn to. We learned some very hard lessons back then. We vowed to help the people so they could help their pets and not have to go through a lot of the heartache like we did.

Flea and tick care can be tricky. So many tick collars are filled with known carcinogens. What do you recommend for flea and tick prevention?

The best way to treat almost all problems is from the inside out. You've certainly heard beauty starts on the inside. Well, good health also starts from the inside. We offer several great safe flea and tick products, both internal and external, to help combat this issue in the safest, healthiest way for not only your pets, but for everyone in the household. Toxic flea products can easily cause problems not only for the pet, but for the people in the household, as well.

Pet owners are becoming more educated. At the very least, most people are avoiding buying pet treats made in China and not buying food with grains and corn. What would you say are other simple steps that we can do for our pets' health when buying food, treats, and products?

First and foremost, learn how to read labels. Incorporate more fresh ingredients in the diet and get yearly wellness checkups. Stop overvaccinating and watch what flea and tick products you use. In other words, become more educated.

Would you say that allergies are the most common canine malady that pet owners are buying remedies for? Why is that? What do you recommend to tackle allergies holistically?

Absolutely one of the highest on the list of problems today is pet allergies, with food being the biggest culprit causing the problems. The easiest and first step is changing the diet.

What do you see are the future trends in this industry? Where would you ideally like to see pet care head?

Trends in the industry are definitely leaning toward fresh, real, wholesome foods. The frozen, raw food market has also grown by leaps and bounds. Also, the increase in online shopping has caused small independent stores to close shop and online marketers to care about profits more than the health of the animals.

I've noticed that numerous giant pet food corporations are buying up the smaller holistic pet food companies that are becoming popular and then vowing to those customers that "nothing will change." Sure enough, ingredients, portion size, and price soon change for the worse. How do you choose some of the brands that you carry? What are you noticing about this trend?

You are absolutely right. Large corporations buy up the smaller companies who became popular because their intentions when formulating their lines were done to help animals become healthier and stronger. Because many of those lines made dents in the sales of the large commercial lines, it makes good business sense to buy them up, change them, and/or get rid of them altogether.

Can you share one of your favorite dog stories?

Thousands of dogs come through our door every day and night. Most of them know exactly how to get to the store even without their owner present. On several occasions, we've had dogs run into the store only to have their owners run in, sometimes hours later! Always with a look of relief on the owners' faces and a look of accomplishment on the dog! We've also helped thousands of pets reach good health again. My own dog Tedi-Anne survived liver cancer, liver resection, spleen removal, canine vestibular disease, and a host of other ailments. She passed at sixteen years old from good, old age.

Follow Whiskers
Facebook: facebook.com/WhiskersHolisticPetcare
Twitter: @WhiskersPets

Kim Freeman

Certified Canine Massage Therapist | CanineMassageTreatment.com

Gaining trust is essential for canine masseuse Kim Freeman when working with her furry clients. She achieves this by always going to the comfort of each dog's home and then making sure that the owner is present, even if they are quietly doing something else in the room. "When their parent is present, it shows that it's okay. It lets the dog know that he or she can begin to trust me." She also wears a white lab coat ("it's a uniform of consistency") and always plays classical, opera, or "spa-like" music. She will never play anything with violins because "it's too high-pitched for dogs."

Freeman says she speaks animal and loves the typical response she gets from the dogs that just "give themselves up to me" and surrender. Licks, heavy sighs, and appreciative glances are her rewards. Whether she is teaching abandoned and abused dogs the power of touch and compassion when she volunteers at a nearby shelter or helping an exhausted new mom of five pups whose milk supply has dried up, Freeman says that the power of massage can be transformational and vital for the well-being of your pet.

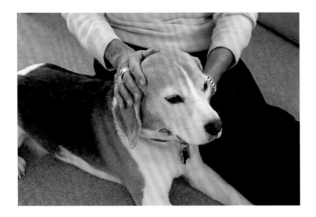

The first consultation at home will be an evaluation of your dog, the reason for the massage, and your dog's medical history. A gentle, head-to-tail "laying of hands" is applied to quiet and calm the client.

Before a front leg stretch, which helps to lengthen muscles and increase blood circulation, the elbow groove and shoulder are warmed up and worked on with a series of strokes. Take note of any spasms.

The evaluation also includes discussing the dog's disposition; posture and comfort level standing, sitting, and lying down; sensitive areas on the body; and exercise habits and daily routine.

Completely relaxed and enjoying the strokes applied to the tummy, the client surrenders to the pleasure of massage.

Massage Tips for Dog Owners

Being patient, calm, loving, and mindful is a priority.

1. We all love petting our dogs, but we usually go only fur deep. Try petting your dog with your palm flat so you just feel its body under your hand, which will give a gentle but more stimulating action, therefore increasing blood circulation, the primary goal of therapeutic massage. In addition, stroking gently with your fingertips in the direction of the muscles will also help with circulation and goes a little deeper than the hand. Try doing this all over the body.

2. Many dogs have sensitive areas as a result of a variety of problems in their past. Some of these are psychological, others medical. With gentle strokes, try for just a few minutes at a time, running your hand over sensitive areas, calmly speaking to your dog, and trying to get his trust. Being patient is very important. Repeat daily or every other day to see if your pet can become more relaxed and trusting with these sensitive areas. This can also prepare him or her for an overall professional massage, a visit to the vet, nail clipping, and grooming.

3. The excited dog. With a low and calm voice, calmly lay your hands on the dog's head or neck and then gently on his back. Continue slowly and gently to lay your hands on his back and down the spine. Repeat a few times.

4. With circular motion and an up-and-down movement like scratching him, rubbing the areas a dog has a hard time getting himself will make him a happy pup. On the scruff of the neck just below the head, under the chin, and on the chest are wonderful feel-good places to do this.

5. Prior to a long walk or playdate, doing any of the above movements will warm up your dog's muscles and help decrease muscle sprain.

6. The more you familiarize yourself with your dog's body, learning his lumps and bumps and sensitive areas, the more knowledgeable and helpful you are to the vet in early detection if something is new or doesn't feel right.

Dr. Marty Goldstein, DVM
Author, *The Nature of Animal Healing* | SmithRidge.com

D r. Marty Goldstein is categorically recognized as *the* pioneer of integrated veterinarian medicine—or what he refers to now as "appropriate medicine"—because he treats each dog individually, starting with a full blood panel and a complete analysis, and then administers subsequent protocol that can range from acupuncture, herbs, supplements, intravenous vitamin C, injectable homeopathic remedies, or cryosurgery. In 1975, after he graduated from Cornell College of Veterinarian Medicine, he became certified in acupuncture and found the ancient Chinese practice to be helpful on a range of animal maladies from pain management to neurological and digestive conditions. At the time, his license was verbally threatened. "I was kind of condemned and deemed insane," he says. Now, acupuncture is one of the most widely accepted complementary therapies across the board on a university and specialty level. "People say to me, 'God, you were so far ahead of your time.' No. I am not ahead of the trends. Its been around for three thousands years. I was thirty years less behind. This is nature." He also discovered the benefits of using Reiki and homeopathy on the animals he treated. "What worked out well for me at the time was that I happened to love photography—I received the photography award at Cornell—and I documented all of my patients." Dr. Marty's philosophy is based in finding and treating the root of the problem, not just treating the symptoms or individual parts. He believes in supporting the body as a whole and naturally boosting the immune system to allow the body to heal. He pragmatically sums it up, "It's about the interconnectedness of all of the organs."

Over four decades of successfully treating thousands of seriously ill pets—many of whom come to his center after their attending veterinarians have delivered a grave prognosis—he has convincing outcomes about the cause of illness as it applies to our canine companions. He's eager to share hefty photo albums of his clinic's most desperate cases that offer optimism to many dog owners who come there as a last hope. Dr. Marty, as he's known to most, has an extensive VIP client list from Oprah

to Martha, a wall of celebrity clients, and a documentary about his life's work coming out next year, but for him, since he "woke up in the seventies as to what disease was really about," he often works up to eighteen-hour days just trying to "keep the vision that one day it would make a difference with the animals."

The Vaccination Link

When Dr. Marty wrote the best seller *The Nature of Animal Healing* almost twenty years ago, he stated that the three most common problems he sees are cancer, arthritis, and conditions of the skin. When asked if those are the top canine maladies he treats today, he replies, "I would say so. A significant cause of allergies—known as *Allergic Breakthrough Phenomena*—is a medical condition that shows the documented link between the enhancement of allergies by vaccinations." Approximately up to 85 percent of all dogs they see at his center have some form of allergy and/or autoimmune condition. For years, Dr. Marty had linked a significant contributing factor to vaccinations, which is now backed up by scientific documentation. "The potency of a vaccine is up to ten times the amount of what a Great Dane would actually need. Besides allergies, there are quite a number of other diseases attributed to documented adverse reactions to vaccinations. Also, it's not just the organism, it's the adjuvant, which makes the vaccine enhance absorption into the body, that is causing more problems than the actual vaccine." He adds, "What vaccines are grown on instigates allergies and autoimmune reactions, which was proven in studies years after my book came out by Purdue and Colorado State. Veterinarians are also seeing a great deal of vaccine-associated sarcoma specifically at the injection sites."

In 2011, The American Animal Hospital Association updated their vaccination guidelines to only core vaccines being needed every three years (with the exception of the legally enforced rabies shots with timing varying state to state). Before they stepped in with their first set of guidelines in 2003, veterinarians only had the pharmaceutical sales reps recommendations to go by. The AAHA acknowledged that even with these updated recommendations, immunity lasts for five years for distemper and parvovirus, and at least seven years for adenovirus—which brings many veterinarians to feel that this apprise, at the very least, is overkill and can pose dangers in vaccinating dogs against diseases they are already immune to. However, some traditional veterinarians are slow to adopt the updated, researched protocol. When asked why, without hesitation, Dr. Goldstein points out, "a good part of veterinarians' incomes comes through giving vaccines. Immune suppression, associated with vaccinations, is one of the main reasons why we see so much cancer." His clinic can see between three to five new cases of canine cancer per day. An increasing number of veterinarians are now doing what he recommends, testing with titers and advocating a protocol that is patient by patient. In addition, he stresses the importance of not giving an ill dog a vaccination, which is often a frequent occurrence with many vets even though the packaging insert on the vaccine says, *Intended for Use On Healthy Animals Only*. "If you give it to a dog with an illness, it is not medically correct."

Fleas, Ticks, and Heartworm

While discussing the latest progress for treating flea and tick prevention from the inside out, Dr. Marty is relieved that the choices and availability for flea and tick prevention have grown tremendously. He supports internal options of naturally occurring herbal blends and a nontoxic bug repellant spray yet also acknowledges the value of conventional prevention when appropriate. "Tick disease is so bad that in areas where it's so heavy, I don't mind certain flea or tick products. I hate chemo and radiation, but we will recommend it *when it's necessary* to buy us more time to work on their immune system in order to get to the root cause of why cancer grew in the first place. Some of the areas here [in the Northeast], you can find thirty to fifty ticks a day. If you are using alternatives, like The Holistic Home Company dog products and internal powders, you don't need a full dose of the heavier practices."

Regarding heartworm, Dr. Marty says if he had a choice, he would rather treat that than the alarming number of cancer-ridden pets he is treating. "I've never given my dog a heartworm pill, and I never will. I've seen three dogs die of heartworm in forty-four years. Last one was 1979. Currently I have treated two dogs in this practice that have had heartworm—one from Texas, one from Mississippi. After putting both on herbal programs, they have been heartworm negative for several years. We don't sell heartworm preventative to over 95 percent of our clients and haven't for almost thirty-five years." Heartworms are spread when a mosquito bites an infected dog and picks up tiny larvae from the dog's bloodstream. Then that mosquito bites another dog, infecting it with the heartworm larvae. He laments the reported adverse reactions of the heartworm preventative. The prevention for a ten-pound dog comes packaged in a box that warns: *If ingested by a human, physicians should call the Poison Control Center immediately.* Dr. Marty often circles back to the benefits of building up the

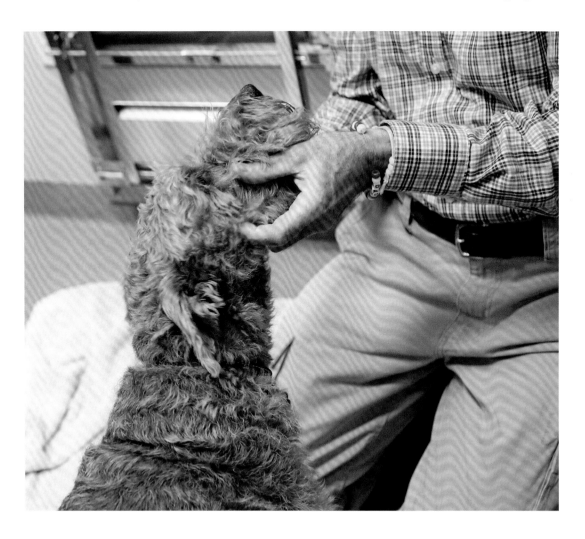

immune system in general, rather than a barrage of chemicals, vaccines, neurotoxins, and carcinogens that weaken it.

"To prevent a disease that I have seen to be treatable, we give a pill [with a list of known side effects], and it says the protection is a minimum forty-five to sixty days. Why are we giving it every thirty days? Why do most vets recommend once a month *year-round*? It is scientifically impossible for heartworm [in northern states] to be active in a mosquito unless it is 57 degrees or higher for twelve to fourteen days in a row. So, if you found a mosquito in your house in January still alive, the chance of it having active heartworm is near zero. I tell my clients that, with my own dogs, if I had a choice of them getting heartworm and treating it, or them taking the prevention—I'd take treating them herbally."

The one exclusion to his rule is if he lived in southern states or especially the Bahamas. "I'd probably give heartworm prevention there because the incidence of it is much greater there than in more northern states. It's about being appropriate. It's appropriate medicine."

Raw versus Kibble

"Nature intended a dog and a cat to eat raw. Period." He does point out, however, that not all dogs can handle raw. There are a great deal of veterinarian raw food advocates out there who agree with Dr. Marty, that dogs with immunosuppressive illness, cancer, or late stage liver or kidney disease have difficulty processing the high-protein raw diets. In the same rational medical manner of his "appropriateness" modus operandi, he is quick to add that "The fundamentals of life are to enjoy it and not live in a glass bubble. If I have salmon for dinner and have some left over, we give it to our dog at home." In addressing the salmonella debate, Dr. Marty quotes the Merck manual that states, ". . . 37 percent of all dogs naturally have salmonella in their intestines. It's an issue of proper sanitation. Do you ever buy raw chicken for your family? Probably. And I'm sure you wash your hands and sanitarily prepare it. Same thing with feeding your pet raw." When asked if he believes that some overly frequent vaccination protocols and feeding kibble will one day be on the list of obsolete practices, he replies, "Hopefully yes, but, it's going to be a long time."

The Soul Connection

Dr. Marty readily understands the soul connection of how dogs come into our lives in a meant-to-be way, or at a much-needed time to teach valuable life lessons. "Oh God, chapter nine of my book! That's why they are in our life. They represent unconditional love." Besides noticing a great deal of owners sharing a physical resemblance with their dogs, he has observed shared commonalities that go even further. "The intra relationship between owners and dogs with disease is uncanny. On a conscious level, the dog's entire life's attention is you. When you also add in a dog's ability with greater perception which has been proven medically—detecting epileptic seizures and certain cancers—you have energy fields that are overlapping in the subconscious or extra physical plane."

That's not to say that your pet will indeed energetically mirror your own health conditions; however, when an owner has a health issue, they should be mindful of keeping a close eye on their pets, as well. He adds, "What you do is, you work on yourself. Step back and look at the entire picture from a holistic perspective. Work on your health, from a mind, body, and spirit perspective, you work on everything."

The Future of Integrative Medicine

As Dr. Marty reflects on the past decades he acknowledges, "Progress has been made. There has been a shift in the pet food industry and in supplementation. Now, fish oils, pre- and probiotics, and milk thistle and joint support supplements are commonly recommended." When discussing future holistic advances, Dr. Marty enthusiastically talks about a tool called the Magna Wave. "In my forty-four years of doing this, I didn't think there would be anything that would get me so excited and change my perspective on therapy. It uses Pulsed Electro Magnetic Frequency. We have a unit here that we have seen shrink some tumors during one treatment." The pulsating magnetic field displaces hydrogen ions, which leads to the normalization of the membrane potential. The cell membrane is able to transport more oxygen and nutrients into the cell. It has been documented that it can enhance the absorption of a medicinal substance up to 200 percent in the area treated. The cell is also able to remove carbon dioxide and other waste products from inside the cell.

PEMF has been used for approximately fifty years to treat pain and swelling, to speed wound healing, and to repair bone fractures in humans (some Olympic athletes reportedly use it), and its use has been widely documented in the equine racing industry. "America's Doctor" Dr. Mehmet Oz calls magnetic therapy "the revolutionary cure for pain that few doctors know about. The FDA has already cleared it for fusing broken bones, treating severe depression, and for treating post-operative pain and swelling. It is changing the practice of medicine."

Dr. Marty is also looking forward to giving credited, integrative veterinary medicine webinars for IDEXX, a popular leader in diagnostic technology that develops innovative analyzing tools and services in his industry. He hopes this medium will allow him to reach a greater peer audience who can then go forward, armed with integrative approaches that are "appropriate" in treating and healing the animals we love so much.

Follow Smithridge Veterinary Center
Facebook: facebook.com/SmithRidge
Twitter: @smithridgevet

Gene Giggleman, DVM

Certified Animal Chiropractor, Parker University, Animal Chiropractic Clinic

Gene Giggleman has been adjusting dogs for more than two decades. He graduated magna cum laude from Texas A & M Veterinarian School, was the dean of academic affairs at Parker University, served as the president of the American Veterinarian Chiropractic Association, and currently he is practicing animal chiropractic and teaching anatomy and toxicology at Parker University, College of Chiropractic.

Most people know the value of chiropractic adjustments for themselves but may not necessarily think of getting their dogs adjusted. When is a good time for a dog to get adjusted?

I recommend all pets receive a chiropractic analysis as soon as six to ten weeks of age. Many issues can be identified and correction can begin at an early age as opposed to waiting until the problem manifests later in life.

Some breeds have a propensity to hip dysplasia. If they receive chiropractic care early on—as a maintenance precaution—will this lessen their chances of having those issues when they get older?

There is no evidenced-based research to this effect, but it has been my experience that identifying laxity in the hip joints early on and starting preventative procedures will lessen the likelihood of developing hip dysplasia. Hip dysplasia is a disease of multifactorial etiologies, and prevention needs to start with breeding out the genetic predisposition. Having said that, all dogs with the genotype for

hip dysplasia do not develop hip dysplasia, and proper supplementation, appropriate chiropractic care, proper nutrition, proper bedding, and controlled exercise will all help in the prevention of developing hip dysplasia disease.

You mentioned bedding. What type is best—a memory foam type of bed?
Typically, soft bedding. I have not read any research to support one type of soft bedding over another, but I would think memory foam would be an excellent choice.

Can you walk us through a typical session?
All pets I see receive a thorough veterinary examination. Once I have completed the exam, I will do an assessment of the dog's musculoskeletal system. I use both static and motion palpation to assess normal ranges of motion of the joints of the pet's body, focusing on the spinal column. I will also do a neurological evaluation on the pet. Once I have determined there is a problem in the motion of a joint, I will adjust that segment using chiropractic techniques. Most dogs and cats respond very favorably to the adjustment, and as soon as I set them down off the table, they run around and act very excited. It takes about fifteen minutes or so to adjust my typical patient.

Can canine chiropractic care help heal the body of other illnesses or diseases? If so, what?
The premise behind chiropractic care is that the nervous system is the master system of the body, and any interference to the nervous system can block the body's innate ability to heal itself. I have seen dogs who have had irritable bowel disease, allergies, seizures, blood disorders, lameness, herniated disc disease, urinary incontinence—just to mention a few—all respond favorably to chiropractic care.

How can an adjustment be extremely beneficial to a dog who has just given birth?
An animal that has given birth undergoes many changes in her body. She may have pelvic or spinal issues that can be helped through chiropractic care. She also may

have special nutritional needs that need to be addressed. I have seen dogs in dystocia (having a difficult time giving birth) benefit from chiropractic care and go on to have a normal delivery. I have seen dogs postpartum have pelvic issues that respond to chiropractic care.

Can it help with lameness?

Many of the animals I treat come to see me because of lameness issues. Obviously, successful treatment depends upon making an accurate diagnosis. An animal with a torn cranial cruciate ligament may benefit from chiropractic care because of the pelvic and spinal issues seen secondary to the lameness caused by the condition but will not be healed by chiropractic care. A complete tear of a cranial cruciate ligament is a surgical issue. So depending upon the cause or the problem, chiropractic care will definitely help dogs with lameness issues. My philosophy is chiropractic first, drugs and surgery second.

Can you share your favorite story about one of your canine patients that you have helped?

I have many, many favorite stories, but I guess my all-time favorite, which was published in the *Chicken Soup for the Chiropractic Soul* book, is about Sparky the Cocker Spaniel. Sparky presented to me with a history of seizures. The dog was on several antiseizure medications, but they were not helping. The owner was frustrated and told me if I could not help the dog, the dog was to be euthanatized. I examined the dog and could find nothing to indicate a cause for seizures, but I did find a firm knot on the dog's right side of its upper neck. You must understand, this is the very first dog I had ever examined from a chiropractic perspective, and I had never adjusted a dog before. I guessed the knot was a subluxation and it caused the dog pain. When I touched it, the dog shivered violently, which the owner told me were the "seizures" the dog was having. I used my adjusting instrument (an Activator®), and since I had no real idea how much force to use, I just turned it up all the way and adjusted the area. The dog collapsed on the table. It scared the heck out of me, and I grabbed the dog and set him on the floor, hoping he could stand and that I had not broken his neck. He stood for a moment, then walked off, stopped, and shook his head, flopping his long ears from side to side as dogs will do. The owner was elated and told me he had not done that in years. I told her to take Sparky home and I would call her the next day to check on him. I called the next day and he was fine, playing with his toys, no more "seizures," and the owner was very happy. Sparky went on to live a long, happy life, and thankfully my first adjustment went very well.

Laura Turley

Dog Walker / Canine Conduct Specialist | DogStarPetsNYC.com

How did you get into this profession? What would you say are your specialties, if any, with canine conduct?

I had worked in the corporate world for years and was at a point where I'd had enough of it. I needed a change. I liked animals, I wanted to be outside and not in an office all day, and I needed work . . . so I started walking dogs for an independent businesswoman. After the third year, I bought the business from her. Now, I do more than just walking. I first started noticing and helping clients with issues and quirks that I noticed their dogs had or that they would tell me about. I focus more on addressing problem behaviors like leash aggression, insecurity, barking excessively, etc., rather than obedience training. My attention is on teaching people how not to just communicate better with their dogs, but also how to better understand what their dogs are saying to them. Humans often misread or project too much of their own rationale onto an animal. My work is often getting people to shift their understanding and their behavior . . . and the behavior of the dog generally follows. Dogs live in the moment. People live in the past or the future, rarely in the moment. Dogs are great for that. They keep you present.

When dealing with aggression in dogs, what would you say are the main causes for that?

That's a trick question. Because I feel like "aggression" is a label that is often misused and misunderstood. The simple answer to the question is there is one common denominator: human beings. It's not always intentional; sometimes humans think they are soothing or trying to help the "aggressive dog," but they are unwittingly doing the opposite and encouraging the aggression. I try to not listen to the human narrative as much as I listen to what the dog is telling me. They are much clearer and also much more willing to snap out of a behavior and forgive and forget than most humans. But for a dog that has had months or even years of getting away with aggressive behavior as a coping mechanism, it takes time and consistency to change it. The owner/handler needs to be committed to changing their own bad habits and to seeing and communicating with their dog differently. Every dog is different; there is not one main cause for "aggression," either toward humans or other dogs, but inconsistent or confusing behavior by their human is almost always a factor.

We know that aggression may be a universal language, but canine-to-human interpretation can be challenging because of species dialectical subtleties that even experienced humans can misread. What are the best ways to handle that behavior?

The best way to handle an aggressive animal of any kind is to be calm. Don't make direct eye contact with an aggressive or barking/snarling dog. That will be read as a challenge and could prompt an attack. It's hard to say the "best way" because it really depends on the situation. Is the dog loose? Restrained? Is it acting aggressively toward another dog or a human? Inside or outside its home? But generally, the calmer and more centered you are, the more likely the dog will calm down.

I've noticed that you use positive enforcement with very calculated timing. Can you tell me more about that?

Well, I wouldn't call it "enforcement." I call it affection. I use it more as a "pat on the back" type thing. I don't give treats every time a dog obeys a command, for instance. "Positive rewards" can mean all sorts of things other than treats or verbal "good boy/ good girl." Dogs have been bred for centuries to please humans—it's instinctual. They are constantly looking at our facial expressions and body language and sensing our emotional states. They are nonverbal communicators. And what most humans forget is that so are we—we just have big egos about our human ability to mouth words. We actually misinform with our words. And that is usually the source of the disconnect in human-dog communications: humans will bark commands, raise their voices, etc., but all the while, their body language is stressed or angry or afraid, and the dog doesn't understand how to respond.

What is the best way to introduce one dog to another?

It's always best to let them sniff butts first. That's how they get to know each other. I call it the "doggie handshake." The nose-to-nose greeting with both dogs out in front of their owners, pulling at the end of the leash—all of that can often set off a challenge between strange dogs, and that can spark barking or snarling or even a fight.

What is the biggest mistake that dog owners make around their dogs?

Not setting boundaries and limitations, and not giving the dog structured exercise. Often what happens is that behaviors that are cute when they are puppies, when left unchecked, become problems and not so cute as the dog becomes older. Suddenly jumping up on you is no longer desirable when your eighty-pound Lab jumps up on a friend's kid and knocks him down.

How do you handle an excessive barker? Why do some dogs bark excessively? How would you recommend handling a neighborhood dog who barks excessively?

It can be a number of things, depending on the dog's environment and humans. Sometimes it's boredom. Sometimes it's for attention or out of anxiety. Most of the time, if you give a dog proper exercise, structured walks, and engagement and then set boundaries and limitations, the dog will not continue disruptive barking.

How can you teach a dog to play nicely with other dogs?

Dogs don't have opposable thumbs, so their mouth is how they grasp at things. So it's natural for them to use their mouths to play. This is not really "biting." When dogs are engaged in play, they give off clear body signals. What humans should get used to doing is recognizing when the excitement level may get too high. Then it's time to check in and slow it down. It's kind of like young kids at play, roughhousing—every parent or babysitter knows that moment when roughhousing reaches a certain frenetic peak, and then someone gets hurt. Hasn't it all happened to us as kids? A responsible parent/human learns to read those signals and *moderate* the energy level of the play. You can slow it down periodically.

Would you say that dogs could be intuitive with their human families?

Dogs are "intuitive" in the same way humans are: they read body language, facial expressions, and so yes, they are constantly taking emotional reads on everyone in the family. Dogs are great empaths. Just the other day, I was having a sad moment and started to tear up a little. A dog I was watching sensed it from across the room and came over and sat on my lap, looking at my face with a worried expression. Instantly. It was a pit, by the way.

Follow Dog Star Pets
Instagram.com/DogStarPets

Dr. Jill Elliot, DVM

Holistic Veterinarian, West Village Veterinarian Hospital | NYHolisticVet.com

For more than twenty years, you have been practicing both conventional and complementary veterinarian medicine with great success on many dogs with chronic or acute problems. Are there ever times when you will categorically only use one modality over the other?

I always look at every case presented to me with both my holistic and conventional hats on and try to determine which is the best way to start the treatment/case. Most of the time, I start with the holistic approach since that is why most owners are seeking my services. If there is no improvement in a short time, I might add some conventional treatments or change the holistic treatment—for instance, change the homeopathic remedy, if they were started on one the first time they came in. I advise my clients that the holistic approach may take a little longer to normalize their pet, but it is worth waiting a little longer to resolve the issues, not just "suppress" the problem, as many conventional medications seem to do.

There are times when I choose to use conventional medicine over holistic. That would be when an animal is very ill and they may need life-saving conventional medicine, which could include fluid therapy, antidiarrhea and antinausea meds, as well as, on occasion, steroids. In vet school, they teach, "never let an animal die without first trying steroids." I have seen animals practically on their deathbeds recover and live a more normal live after introducing steroids into their treatment regime. However, I usually try, whenever possible, to start with holistic medications and treatments, sometimes along with conventional meds or treatments.

In cases of animals with musculoskeletal issues that may or may not have seen a neurologist (often suggested by their conventional vet), I will suggest chiropractic (VOM) and low-level (cold) laser (LLL) series of treatments. I have seen these two modalities totally turn around animals with serious and not-so-serious conditions. In these cases, if the animal is in a lot of pain, I will add some pain meds for a short

time. Many times, these animals can get off these pain meds after a few VOM and LLL treatments.

Allergies and skin conditions seem to be some of the most common canine maladies today. How can a dog owner accurately assess and treat these issues at home using homeopathy?

Allergies and skin issues are rampant and very frustrating to treat. There are many homeopathic remedies considered "acute" remedies. Owners can start using some of these to see if there is any improvement in their pets' conditions. There are many books that can help owners decide which remedies to try first even before seeking professional help.

However, skin issues can be considered a "constitutional issue" by many homeopaths. This means it is more than an acute problem and might require a more in-depth analysis from a veterinary homeopath. That person would be trying to find the "constitutional remedy" that would fit the whole picture of the animal—not just the skin condition—and give a remedy based on that.

My rule of thumb with using remedies for acute conditions is to give it three or four times (in one day or over two days). If the condition does not improve, try a different remedy. In emergency situations, like a vaccine/allergic reaction that could be life-threatening, the owner can be giving a remedy frequently (every five seconds) while they are on the way to their vet. The animal's condition might even resolve by the time they get to the vet's office. But it should still be checked out and evaluated by the vet.

I crush up homeopathic pills for my dog's allergies and put the powder in my hand for him to lick. He goes for it each time. I avoid giving him food or water for thirty minutes afterward. Is this the best manner to dispense this regimen?

The method you describe is fine. Remedies are absorbed from the mucus membranes. Therefore, as long as the pet's mouth doesn't have food in it, it is okay to give it. It's not necessary to wait thirty minutes for feeding, though. My suggested method of giving remedies to pets is to dissolve three to five pellets in half a glass (four ounces) of bottled/filtered water. Stir thirty seconds. Then put a syringeful or teaspoonful of the mixture on the pet's gums. It does not have to be swallowed. It is immediately absorbed. You can reuse this mixture as needed for a few days. DO NOT REFREGERATE MIXTURE. Refrigerators have electromechanical energy that can "knock off" the effect of the homeopathic remedy (since the remedy works on an energetic level). You don't need more than three to five pellets for any dose. More pellets is not a stronger dose.

You use veterinary low-level (cold) lasers for treating many issues including muscular skeletal, diabetes, allergies, digestive issues, and much more. Can you tell us more about this tool, when it's most useful, and what can be expected in a session?

The LLL is an amazing tool. I have been using it for approximately seven years and have seen miracles with this treatment. I have seen paralyzed animals walk. I have seen large dogs with arthritis that had to be pulled along by their owners before a session who then pull their owner to go home after a session. I use it mostly for musculoskeletal issues such as arthritis, disc disease, joint pain, limping, rear end weakness, degenerative joint disease, hip dysplasia, etc. These conditions all seem to improve. About 85 percent of the dogs I see with these conditions get better with a series of treatments. Many can reduce or discontinue their pain medications.

In addition to all of the above, LLL can be used to treat allergies, skin problems, digestive issues (IBD), focus problems for geriatric animals, and many other issues. The total session is approximately fifteen minutes. The pet does not feel anything when lights are shined on them.

Six Easy Ways to Enhance Your Dog's Health

- Tap the dog's chest (breast bone) gently ten times a day to wake up the seat of immunity. That is where the thymus gland lives. As animals age, the thymus gland shrinks.
- Brushing the dog's teeth daily and brushing the whole animal daily is a good ritual to establish if possible (with animals that will allow it). Keeps teeth clean longer, prevents tartar buildup, and avoids dental cleanings with anesthesia if done religiously. Brushing the coat removes dead skin and hair and wakes up the circulation in the skin to keep it healthier.
- Give supplements like Omega 3, 6, 9 to help build up immunity. Probiotics are great for GI as well as mental focus and agility. As animals age, the owner should give a good all-around vitamin supplement.

- Feed a variety of proteins. Many pet owners just feed chicken. Animals fed the same protein for a long time can become allergic to that specific protein. It's good to mix it up. If feeding processed food, feed ones that do not say they have byproducts on the label.
- Take your dog to the vet at least once a year for checkup to catch any problems. With middle-aged and older animals, visits twice a year with complete blood and urine tests help to find problems early.
- Do not overvaccinate. Request blood tests (titers) to be done instead of yearly vaccines after the age of five.

Dental care can be bothersome to maintain regularly, yet if there is a problem, it can become very costly. Do you have any tips for easy at-home care?

Dental care of pets' teeth is very important if the pet will allow it. You can brush their teeth with pet toothpaste and, using a toothbrush or a gauze pad wrapped around your finger, brushing or rubbing gently on their gum line and the tops of their teeth.

Don't worry about the bottom teeth. Concentrate on the top teeth in front and sides of mouth. Put a supplement like Perio Support into pets' food twice a day. This is a mineral supplement that helps to take tartar off teeth if used regularly. There are many other oral products that can be used—gels, oral rinses, etc. Owners should have this discussion with their vets early in their pet's life or as soon as they realize it's part of good care. Some pets just won't allow anyone to put anything in their mouths. In these cases, perhaps a good marrowbone to chew on for one hour a day might work with dogs. And of course there are commercial products to help clean teeth when chewed, like Greenies, to name just one.

Many scientific and academic studies are revealing alarming side effects regarding overvaccinating. What precautions do you take with vaccinations? Are there any that can be completely avoided?

Too many vaccines are given too often, which is not good for most pets. Every vaccine causes an inflammatory response in the pet to create the antibodies needed to cause protection. The manufacturer of most vaccines puts a slip in their box of vaccines that states, "Only vaccinate healthy animals." Unfortunately, many vets continue to revaccinate animals with acute and serious chronic diseases, like hyperthyroid and hypothyroid disease, heart disease, allergies, irritable bowel disease, and respiratory diseases, to name a few. I don't vaccinate these animals. Instead, I recommend they get a blood test called a titer. This measures the antibody level and tells us whether the animal has adequate protection. I use this for distemper/parvo, and you can also do it for rabies. If an animal has a serious medical condition, I suggest these titers. Even if they don't have a serious medical condition, after they turn five, I suggest doing titers for distemper and parvo. Usually, the animal shows they have protection for three to four years after the vaccine is given. If the titer shows that there is not adequate protection to either of these, you can ask your vet to only vaccine for the one that is not adequate. Drug manufacturers do sell single-dose vaccines for distemper and parvo. Since the rabies titer is rather expensive in some places and rabies vaccine is a matter of law, I do recommend it every three years (but not more often) if needed.

Post-vaccines, there are some homeopathic remedies that can "take away or reduce" any negative reactions from vaccines. I recommend giving Lyssen 200c once a day for two days after the rabies vaccines and Thuja 200c once a day for two days after any other vaccine. (Three pellets dissolved in a half glass of water. Give a teaspoon of the mixture into the pet's mouth once a day for two days from the same mixture. Do not refrigerate.)

All the other vaccines recommended by veterinarians should be discussed. I usually make my assessment of which other vaccines might be needed depending on the pet's lifestyle. Are they mainly a city dog, just walk around the block and go home? Do they stay in the house most of the time? Do they go to the park daily and play with other dogs at the dog run? Do they go to doggie day care and are exposed to many dogs? All these factors are taken into effect to decide which, if any, additional vaccines are needed.

Can you please share your personal favorite heartwarming dog story?

Randy, a two-year-old, black neutered male Cocker Spaniel had been in terrible back pain and had just had back surgery. Unfortunately, after the surgery the dog was paralyzed. The owners were devastated. They heard about the success with my patient Gus, a one-year-old Havanese, whom I was treating with cold laser and chiropractic and wanted me to see their dog to see if there was anything holistic I could do. Randy was indeed paralyzed in his rear legs. I advised them that we should try laser only, since he had a bulge on his back over the area that had had surgery. We started doing two lasers twice a week for the first and second weeks, then one laser weekly. The owner used to bring Randy to see me in his SUV and didn't want to have to move Randy around a lot, so I used to do the treatments in the back seat of the SUV. After six treatments, the owner took Randy out of the car when we finished the treatment and stood him up on the ground while he fixed the blanket in the car before putting Randy back. To both our amazement, Randy started to walk down the sidewalk away from the car. The owner retrieved Randy quickly, and we hugged each other out of joy! Randy continued his treatments with me until we completed twelve laser treatments.

Homeopathic Remedy Suggestions for Emergency and Acute Situations

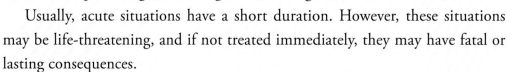

Definition of Acute Illness: Physical or mental condition that has a sudden onset. This may be a condition that happens to the body, e.g., trauma (falls, hit by car, etc.), bite wound (animal, insect, etc.), poisoning (food, drugs, etc.), or fright (shock, stress, etc.).

Usually, acute situations have a short duration. However, these situations may be life-threatening, and if not treated immediately, they may have fatal or lasting consequences.

If you think that your pet is experiencing a life-threatening condition, immediately take him/her to the closest veterinary office that is open (hopefully, your regular vet). On the way to the office, you can try giving the appropriate remedy indicated for the condition. If there's no positive response to the remedy you have chosen after three to four doses, try another remedy. However, you may stop giving the remedy as soon as you see signs of improvement.

How to Give the Remedies:

Purchase remedies in 30C potency unless otherwise indicated. This is strong enough for most acute problems. A "dose" would consist of "3 pellets" directly into your animal's mouth. (These pellets are the size of peppercorns). Remedies can be diluted in a half glass of filtered or bottled water. Give ½–1 teaspoon of the mixture from this dilution as a dose into your dog's/cat's mouth. All remedies should be given without food and ideally 10 minutes after your pet has consumed food so that their mouth is clean. These remedies get absorbed into the mucus membranes. It does not have to be swallowed. The pellets or liquid just needs to make contact with the dog's gums or mucus membranes. If you cannot give the remedy to the dog through its mouth for various reasons, you can also pour, squirt, or dip a cotton ball into liquid and rub on their ear or skin (hairless part) or on a clean vulva or anus.

Trauma:

(Accidents, falls, hit by car, postsurgery, emotional shock, pains from over-exertion, etc.)

- **Arnica montana (200C or 1M):** This is the first remedy to reach for in any of the above situations. It's like homeopathic aspirin. It has an excellent calming effect for any acute trauma to the body or mind. In an emergency, it can be repeated frequently; for pains of over-exertion, repeat 3 to 4 times a day. If you only have 30C, give that.
- Be aware that when an animal is in pain, even the sweetest animal, it may bite you when you reach out to it. *Be very careful* when you give the remedy or try to pick your dog up. Use your coat or a blanket if you have one to pick up the pet.

- **Aconitum napellus:** Give this remedy immediately. It will help with shock, especially if the condition has a sudden onset. A1M dose one time is recommended. If you only have 30C, give that.
- **Rescue Remedy:** This is not a homeopathic remedy; it is a Bach Flower Essence. However, it is very helpful in promoting a feeling of well-being after physical or emotional trauma. (Give 5 to 10 drops in water or, if in spray form, 2 sprays, directly into the animal's mouth or on anus.) These two treatments can be used together at the same time. Repeat as frequently as needed. You can also use these anytime you think your pet might experience anxiety or fear.

Allergic Conditions: Anaphylaxis, Vaccine Reactions and Bites & Stings (animals, insects, etc.)

Allergic reactions may cause vomiting, diarrhea, collapse, difficulty breathing, swelling around the face and tongue, as well as pale mucous membranes (gums). This is a life-threatening situation. Rush your pet to the vet and give the remedy on the way.

- **Apis mellifica (200C or 1M preferred):** Give this remedy if you see bright red swelling, facial swelling, swelling around any wound. May look like hives (vaccine reaction/bee sting). If you only have 30C, give it.
- **Cantharis:** Give when bites/stings become inflamed, looks like a burn, blister.
- **Lachesis:** Use if area around bite/sting turns purple/red and painful.
- **Ledum palustre:** First choice for bites/strings/puncture wounds, unless another remedy is better indicated. The area may feel cold to touch but gets better with cold compresses.

Burns from Hot Water, Stove, Scalds, and Sunburns:
- **Arsenicum album:** Animal seems chilly, restless, and thirsty. Worse after midnight. Wound swollen, +/- infected, ulcerated, painful.

- **Cantharis:** First remedy for sunburn, scalds. Give it immediately. Best before blister forms, but try even if blistered.
- **Urtica urens:** If applied topically (tincture form), it can reduce pain and inflammation of first-degree burns. Burns are itching and painful. This remedy can also be taken orally (homeopathically).
- **Calendula ointment or cream:** Apply topically to reduce pain and inflammation, as well. (This is not supposed to be ingested by pets.)

For Skin Rashes, Wounds, and Skin Infections:
- **Calendula ointment or cream:** Apply topically three to four times a day. This is excellent and will prevent bacterial growth on area where applied.

Acute Vomiting/Regurgitation:
- **Arsenicum album:** Vomiting and diarrhea together. Animal is restless, seeking warmth, thirsty. Extreme cases: weakness with collapse, with coldness. Bad smell to vomit. Vomiting may be painful (cats that cry before vomiting).
- **Bismeth:** Similar to Arsenicum, but more intense. Stomach pain, pronounced. Clingy to owner. Seeking cold water, vomits immediately after drinking.
- **Ipecacuanha:** Nausea and vomiting with respiratory condition. Often brought on by overeating +/- blood in vomit.
- **Nux vomica:** For poisoning with garbage, overeating, other toxic causes, especially drug reactions. Animal is seeking warmth and irritable. May have painful vomiting. Feels better after vomiting.
- **Phosphorous:** Regurgitation rather than vomiting. Food brought up immediately after eating or drinking. Ravenous appetite, eating too quickly. Thirsty, prefers cold water. Animal tends to be thin, friendly, and vocal.
- **Pulsatilla:** Thirstless and vomiting undigested food several hours after eating. Animal craves attention and has sweet disposition. Usually seeking warmth or fresh air.

- **Veratrum album:** Life-threatening violent vomiting, with collapse and coldness. *Needs immediate veterinary care.* Good for food poisoning. Give this remedy on the way to the vet's office.

Car/Motion/Sea Sickness:
- **Cocculus:** Give one dose before getting in car. Then as needed while riding.

Diarrhea:
- **Aloe:** Urine and feces passes together with gas. Sudden urges to pass stool, may not make it to the litter box. Worse in early morning, forcing animal to wake up to defecate. Mentally: sad in the morning, cheerful in the evening. Tires easily.
- **Arsenicum album:** Parvovirus—extreme weakness. Foul-smelling diarrhea. Black or very watery; anus may become red. Much straining. Diarrhea and vomiting may occur at the same time. Mentally: restless, thirsty, seeking warmth.
- **Baptisia:** Parvovirus and infections of blood and intestine if symptoms match. Rapid debilitation and severe prostration. *Needs immediate vet care.* (Give remedy on the way to vet's office.) Offensive, watery, bloody diarrhea. *Gums dark.*
- **Colocynthis:** Jelly-like mucous in diarrhea and gas. Stool may contain white shreds. Least food or drink will cause evacuation. Extreme abdominal pain. Animal may lie on stomach or curl up to try to relieve pain. Slight touch causes pain leading to crying or moaning.
- **Lycopodium clavatum:** Intestinal problems (as well as history of urinary problems—not necessarily at the same time). Excessive gas. Animal prefers to be in the same room with owner but not seeking attention. Diarrhea associated with chronic liver disease.
- **Mercurius (vivus or solubulis):** Straining present, especially after passing stool. Stool contains blood and mucous. May strain for urination, too.

- **Nux vomica:** Constipation may alternate with diarrhea. Animal may have had lots of drugs in past history. Especially for food poisoning, garbage eating. Animal may be irritable.
- **Phosphorous:** Parvovirus. Foul-smelling diarrhea with blood. Bleeding and prostration of anus (with anus partially open). Mentally: nervous, skittish, demanding/vocal for food and attention.
- **Podophyllum:** Painless, profuse, bad-smelling stool, possibly yellow or greenish. After much diarrhea, animal may become exhausted.
- **Pulsatilla:** Stool changes, may alternate with constipation. Animal is sweet and want food and attention.
- **Sulphur:** Diarrhea forces animal out of bed in early morning. Anus may be red with pain on defecation. Mentally: lazy. May feel hot, seek cool places, and look unkempt.
- **Veratrum album:** This animal *needs immediate vet care*. You will see severe diarrhea, coldness, weakness, and collapse. Intense purging from both ends simultaneously. (Give remedy on the way to vet office.) Gums may be blue.

Cystitis:

Frequent urging to urinate, with straining, and usually blood in urine. If your dog cannot pass urine, it is an emergency situation. *Immediate veterinary care is needed.* (However, try giving the indicated homeopathic remedies on the way to the vet's office.)

- **Aconitum napellus:** Mentally, the animal is extremely anxious, fearful. May run and hide or seem frantic. Best used early in the course of disease.
- **Belladonna:** Mentally, the animal may appear wild, with dilated pupils. May have a fever. May bite if approached or touched.
- **Lycopodium:** History of diarrhea and gas. Timid or bossy animals with cystitis.
- **Nux vomica:** Mentally, the animal may be irritable, withdrawn, and adverse to company. May have a history of conventional drugs used.

- **Pulsatilla:** Sweet, gentle animal seeking affection, with a tendency to urinate involuntarily at times. Worse when lying down.
- **Sarasaparilla:** Painful at end of urination. Tends to stand up to urinate. Animal may cry at end of urination. May happen after a chill.
- **Thlaspi bursa pastoris:** Chronic cystitis attacks, especially with phosphate crystals. Sediment looks like red brick dust. *Useful for unblocking urethral obstructions.* (Give on the way to vet office.)
- **Thuja occidentalis:** Problems started after (but not necessarily immediately after) vaccine administration. (If none of the other remedies work, try one dose of 30C of this remedy.) If condition improves, consult a homeopathic veterinarian for treatment of the chronic disease.
- **Urtica urens:** Frequent urging, little urine passed. Animal exhausted from trying. May have crystals or bladder stones. May be itchy in general.

NOTE: If the seemingly indicated remedy has not acted (after 4 doses), try one of the others until you've gone through all of them. This problem may reoccur without treatment of the underlying problem.

Bleeding:
- **Phosphorous:** Repeat every 5 minutes for three doses until bleeding stops.
- **Hamamelis:** Passive venous congestion. Bruising and soreness at site.
- **Lachesis:** If phosphorous doesn't work, give this remedy if you see blue tissue near site of bleeding.

Injuries To Nerves:
- **Hypericum:** Injuries to nerve centers and tissues (especially areas rich in nerves like fingertips). Good for back/neck injuries and pain. Excellent to give after dental work with extractions.

Eyes: (give remedies orally not in the eyes)
- **Apis:** Red puffy eyes with watery tears.
- **Euphrasia:** Eyes bloodshot, red, burning, itching. Photophobia, with or without discharge.
- **Belladonna:** with dilated pupils.
- **Optique 1** (Homeopathic eye drops—1 to 2 drops in affected eye/s for 3 to 5 days): Any redness; itchy eyes; conjunctivitis (not for corneal ulcers).

Inhalation of Gas or Other Material:
- **Silicea 6x (cell/tissue salts):** Can be taken after inhalation of foreign material to clean the lungs. Take 4 tablets 3 times a day.
- **Silicea 30C:** Helps to expel small foreign material from the body.

Postsurgical Regime
(Give these all 3 of these remedies for one week postsurgical situation as indicated below)
- **Arnica 30C:** 3 pellets morning
- **Staphysagria 30C:** 3 pellets midday
- **Calendula 30C:** 3 pellets evening

Postdentistry:
- **Arnica 30C:** 3 pellets 2 times a day for 1 to 2 days.
- **Hypericum 3OC:** 3 pellets once a day in addition to the Arnica if any extractions were done. This remedy helps to heal any nerve damage/pain.

Homeopathic treatment for any ongoing, chronic disease is best done under the guidance of a homeopathic veterinarian. Dr. Jill Elliot is not responsible for any conditions or problems that may arise from the use of the above-suggested remedies in the previous pages herewith.

These suggestions were compiled from her clinical practice experiences as well as taken from *Homeopathic Care of Dogs and Cats*, by Don Hamilton, DVM. Additional information was taken from seminars given by Richard Pitcairn, DVM, PhD.

Follow Dr. Jill Elliot
Twitter: @Petdrjill

Gerald Post, DVM, MEM, DACVIM (Oncology)
Chief Medical Officer, Veterinary Cancer Center | VccHope.com

The Veterinary Cancer Center is a referral-based practice that is one of the largest stand-alone cancer facilities in the country. They see between fifteen and forty dogs per day and are known for their integrated team approach in treating both the client and their pet. Even the thoughtful design of the facility itself takes into consideration the needs of a grieving pet owner with a side door for a "compassion room." The doctors don't wear lab coats because "the dogs don't like them," and an open room layout gives the dogs a comforting assurance that they are a part of the pack.

I hate to start off on a grim note, but the recent statistics are sobering. According to recent studies, 50 percent of all dogs will have cancer in their lifetime and 50 percent of dogs over ten[8] will die from it. Strictly from a *prevention perspective*, what, if anything, can dog owners do to lessen the odds of their dog getting cancer? Evidence is mounting that, at least for certain types of cancers, owners can decrease the risk of cancer occurring in their dog. Physicians have known for years that good nutrition and adequate exercise are very important in maintaining our (human) health. Veterinarians are finding that the same advice holds true for our dogs (and cats), as well.

Early detection is also extremely important. Researchers have shown that finding cancerous lesions before they become malignant or while they are still small and removable can prevent many cancers from becoming life-threatening.

The newest bit of research comes out of the venerable MD Anderson Cancer Center in Texas. Researchers there concluded that the use of nonsteroidal anti-inflammatory

---

8 "Cancer and Your Pets: What You Need to Know," Texas A&M University. Veterinary Medicine & Biomedical Sciences, December 2008, at http://vetmed.tamu.edu/news/pet-talk/cancer-and-your-pets-what-you-need-to-know

drugs, or NSAIDs, is linked to a significant decrease in the incidence of certain cancers. Previous research published in one of the leading medical journals, *The Lancet*, demonstrated that taking low doses of aspirin—once daily for at least five years—decreases the chance of a person getting lung, GI, or colon cancer. Although the research was evaluated in people, dogs (and cats) respond similarly to NSAIDs.

Basically, NSAIDs inhibit a group of enzymes in the body, some of which cause inflammation. Inflammation, especially acute inflammation, is essential for wound healing and other important immune functions. When inflammation becomes chronic in nature, cancer risk increases. Cancer seems to be able to co-opt the cells involved in this process and utilize them to allow malignant cells to proliferate.

Therefore, NSAIDs and other compounds that decrease or stop chronic inflammation may be able to prevent cancer in our pets. Cruciferous vegetables (e.g., kale and broccoli) along with yellow, orange, and red vegetables decrease inflammation, specifically by decreasing the levels of prostaglandin E2 in the body. Evidence suggests that feeding dogs these types of vegetables at least three times per week can decrease the risk of bladder cancer in certain breeds.

There are risks to the gastrointestinal tract, kidneys, and liver from the chronic administration of NSAIDs to dogs. Consult your veterinarian to assess the benefits of cancer prevention against the possible side effects of these medicines. Giving your dog vegetables, however, comes with little to no risk—unless of course, your dog feels the way I do about cauliflower.

The level of evidence for low-carbohydrate diets benefiting cancer patients is growing. Most malignant cells, unlike normal cells, require a steady source of glucose (a simple carbohydrate) in the blood to grow and proliferate and are not able to utilize significant amounts of fat due to abnormalities within the mitochondria of the tumor cells. In regard to pets that already have cancer, a low-carbohydrate diet is likely beneficial, but the evidence is circumstantial, especially if the cancer is in an advanced stage. When it comes to cancer prevention, the evidence is more robust.

Turmeric is a spice grown in tropical Asia and used extensively as an herbal remedy in India, Indonesia, and China. The active ingredient, curcumin, is found in the roots and rhizomes of the herb. Cumin, a spice made from the seeds of a different plant, is not related to curcumin. According to the American Cancer Society, curcumin is an antioxidant, and studies evaluating its effectiveness in cancer prevention and treatment show promising results. There is one study showing the benefit of curcumin in people with lymphoma and another study showing improvement in general health and cachexia in people with colorectal cancer. Unfortunately, curcumin is not well absorbed by the gastrointestinal tract, and it can affect the metabolism of many medications including chemotherapeutic drugs, so care must be used when giving this drug to a pet already on medication. Much, if not most, of the current data are preclinical at this point, so the level of evidence about its effectiveness in cancer prevention or treatment is low.

Omega-3 fatty acids (also called fish oil, marine oil, cod liver oil) are important nutrients that the body is unable to make and must be acquired through food. Recent evidence shows that omega-3 fatty acid supplements can improve the efficacy of some chemotherapy drugs and improve survival in people with certain cancers. Perhaps the strongest evidence to date that these nutrients may help prevent cancer is the fact that omega-3 fatty acids have strong anti-inflammatory effects, and chronic inflammation is one of primary causes of cancer. Regarding detrimental effects, there is evidence that omega-3 fatty acid supplementation affects platelets and clotting. However, clinically, these animals don't seem to develop a bleeding problem.

Vitamin D has a protective effect against colon cancer according to many, but not all, studies. The evidence for the protective effect of vitamin D on most cancers (other than colon cancer) is inconclusive. Excessive doses of vitamin D can be very harmful by increasing the level of calcium in the body and causing kidney damage or even failure. So, if you choose to use vitamin D, please do so with care and monitor your dog's calcium level.

Vitamin E is a fat-soluble nutrient that has antioxidant properties. Early observational studies pointed to a protective effect against certain cancers. In 2008, a very well-designed study involving more than 35,000 men concluded that rather than protecting men against prostate cancer, vitamin E (and selenium, another related

antioxidant) supplementation increased the risk of prostate cancer. This finding was again validated in 2011 and 2014. At this time, vitamin E supplementation is not recommended to prevent cancer.

Vitamin A is a fat-soluble nutrient. Currently, the evidence for a protective effect of vitamin A supplementation is inconclusive. In one study involving almost 20,000 people, there was a significant reduction of cancer in people taking vitamin A supplements. However, in another study of almost 30,000 people, no beneficial effect was found.

Vitamin C, though not technically a preventative, has been touted as a cancer treatment for many years. The question that has not been answered is whether high-dose vitamin C given intravenously is helpful in the treatment of cancer. The evidence is inconclusive regarding the effectiveness of vitamin C as a therapy, either when used alone or in combination with chemotherapy or radiation therapy.

The amount of information about veterinary nutrition is rapidly increasing. Board-certified veterinary nutritionists are the experts and likely the best people to ask for the most up-to-date information about cancer prevention using diets or supplements. Many veterinary schools and some private practices have nutritionists on staff.

There have been some studies[9] that suggest overvaccinating can lead to certain types of cancers. What are your thoughts on that? Are annual boosters necessary?
Vaccines are designed to protect our pets and prevent disease. Yet over the past twenty years, veterinarians have come to understand that vaccines can also cause cancer, which is a problem identified in cats much more commonly than in dogs. This has made the decision about whether to vaccinate a pet a difficult and challenging one.

Vaccines still are important to protect our pets from infectious diseases, such as rabies, parovirus, Bordetella, distemper, panleukopenia, feline leukemia virus, rhinotracheitis, and calicivirus.

The best advice is to vaccinate your pet against the diseases that he or she is realistically exposed to. This means that if you live in a high-rise apartment and your cat or dog never goes outside, the risks of exposure to many of these infectious diseases is quite small. The other piece of advice that I give to pet parents is to vaccinate only as frequently as needed and no more. For example, current research suggests that many vaccines provide protection for several years, so these vaccines should be boosted no more than once every three years.

There is also some evidence that the adjuvant in the vaccine is one of the components that can lead to excessive inflammation and potentially to cancer formation. Therefore, using nonadjuvanted vaccines may be helpful.
Weighing the risks of vaccination against the risks of not vaccinating your pet is important. It is becoming increasingly important for you and your veterinarian

---

[9]   "Effects of Vaccination on the Endocrine and Immune Systems of Dogs, Phase II," Purdue University, November 1, 1999, at http://www.homestead.com/vonhapsburg/haywardstudy onvaccines.html.

to discuss the unique set of factors that affect your pet. The decisions that each pet parent makes may be different based upon their circumstances.

Besides feeling a lump, a loss of appetite, lethargy, and bleeding, are there any other suspicious signs that should be examined for a possibility of cancer?
The earlier you detect cancer, the better your chance of effective treatment. Below are ten warning signs of cancer I developed for the Animal Cancer Foundation (www.acfoundation.org). Please understand that these are just potential warning signs and should not panic you, but rather prompt a visit to your veterinarian.

1. **Swollen lymph nodes:** These "glands" are located all throughout the body but are most easily detected behind the jaw or behind the knee. When these lymph nodes are enlarged, they can suggest a common form of cancer called lymphoma. A biopsy or cytology of these enlarged lymph nodes can aid in the diagnosis.

2. **An enlarging or changing lump:** Any lump on a pet that is rapidly growing or changing in texture or shape should have a biopsy. Lumps belong in biopsy jars, not on pets.

3. **Abdominal distension:** When the "stomach" or belly becomes rapidly enlarged, this may suggest a mass or tumor in the abdomen or it may indicate some bleeding that is occurring in this area. A radiograph or an ultrasound of the abdomen can be very useful.

4. **Chronic weight loss:** When a pet is losing weight and you have not put your pet on a diet, you should have your pet checked. This sign is not diagnostic for cancer but can indicate that something is wrong. Many cancer patients have weight loss.

5. **Chronic vomiting or diarrhea:** Unexplained vomiting or diarrhea should prompt further investigation. Often, tumors of the gastrointestinal tract can cause chronic vomiting and/or diarrhea. Radiographs, ultrasound examinations, and endoscopy are useful diagnostic tools when this occurs.

6. **Unexplained bleeding:** Bleeding from the mouth, nose, penis, vagina, or gums that is not due to trauma should be examined. Although bleeding disorders do occur in pets, they usually are discovered while pets are young. If unexplained bleeding starts when a pet is old, a thorough search should be undertaken.

7. **Cough:** A dry, nonproductive cough in an older pet should prompt chest radiographs to be taken. This type of cough is the most common sign of lung cancer. Please remember there are many causes of cough in dogs.

8. **Lameness:** Unexplained lameness, especially in large or giant breed dogs, is a very common sign of bone cancer. Radiographs of the affected area are useful for detecting cancer of the bone.

9. **Straining to urinate:** Straining to urinate and blood in the urine usually indicate a common urinary tract infection; if the straining and bleeding are not rapidly controlled with antibiotics or are recurrent, cancer of the bladder may be the underlying cause. Cystoscopy or other techniques that allow a veterinarian to take a biopsy of the bladder are useful and sometimes necessary to establish a definitive diagnosis in these cases.

10. **Oral odor:** Oral tumors do occur in pets and can cause a pet to change its food preference (e.g., from hard to soft foods) or cause a pet to change the manner in which it chews its food. Many times, a foul odor can be detected in pets with oral tumors. A thorough oral examination with radiographs or CT scan, requiring sedation, is often necessary to determine the cause of the problem.[10]

Where do you see the future of canine cancers?

The future of veterinary oncology is incredibly exciting. Immuno-oncology and genomics are the two big advances that are on the horizon. Within the field of immune-oncology, checkpoint inhibitors have revolutionized the treatment of

---

10. Reprinted with permission from *Animal Fair Magazine*. Visit at animalfair.com.

many human cancers and are being actively developed for veterinary use. Certainly genomics—whether it be sequencing of tumors or gene expression analysis (www.innogenics.com)—are here and being used in veterinary medicine. Advances are being made faster and in more areas now than I have seen in the past thirty years. It is a wonderful time to be a veterinary oncologist. Although my biggest wish is that at some point, there will not be a need for oncologists.

You work at the Veterinary Cancer Center, which is the largest stand-alone veterinary oncology center in the world. Your website is full of inspiring success stories. Can you share one of your favorite success stories with us?
My favorite story is my own dog, Smokey's. Smokey, my miniature schnauzer, was more than a pet to me—he was my constant companion. For fifteen years, we shared our lives, and his passing on May 21, 2005, was one of the saddest days of my life. But as horrible as that day was, it will always be overshadowed by the fifteen years of utter happiness. No matter what went wrong (or right) in my life, Smokey was always with me, and his presence and love got me through many tough times. We truly shared our lives; it was always Gerry and Smokey together, never Gerry and Smokey alone.

Smokey was always excited to see me. (How many people in your lives are always glad to see you?) Whether I was gone for an hour or two weeks, when I walked through my front door, I knew I would hear his bark as he came running toward me. As most pet owners know, this welcome home is one of the great joys of being a dog owner. And in truth, I was always equally glad to see him!

Smokey, my Smokey-dog, my companion, was truly a constant source of happiness. Smokey spent the first ten weeks of his life at my side. During the day, we went to Central Park to play, and at night we both worked at a local emergency hospital (I was on the late-night shift at a veterinary hospital). For the next fifteen years, Smokey saw me through a residency in oncology, studying for boards, board certification, multiple moves across country, and countless other trying times in my life. The unique bond I shared with him can never be broken or duplicated.

I think the hardest thing Smokey had to do in his life was share me. For eleven years, he had to share me with my partner, David, and for the past nine years with our other pet, Cody. Sharing was never one of Smokey's strong points (as both David and Cody can attest), but he did come to love both David and Cody very much.

Smokey was diagnosed with metastatic melanoma after I noticed a tiny cut on one of his toes; a biopsy of the toe and a radiograph of his lungs showed that the melanoma of his toe had already spread to his lungs. When I saw the radiographs and read the biopsy report, I was devastated, as I knew that the average survival time of dogs with this type of cancer was about three months. As Smokey was incredibly healthy and vibrant at this time, and I was unwilling to lose him, I contacted everyone I knew in the veterinary and human oncology fields to try and come up

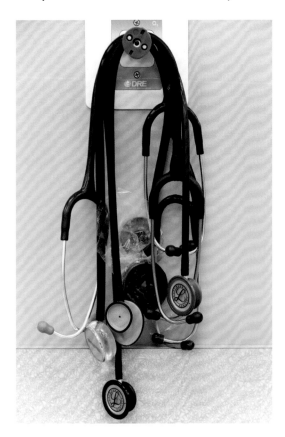

with a treatment plan that would save him. We put him on two courses of one experimental vaccine with chemotherapy, which miraculously caused the tumor in his lungs to shrink, then remain stable for an amazing nine months. We then put him on a third experimental vaccine, which slowed his tumor's growth rate for another twelve months. Smokey's tumor then started growing again. By this time in his life, he also started to develop weakness in his rear legs, likely the result of intervertebral disc disease. Two and a half years after the initial diagnosis, we unfortunately had to put Smokey to sleep due to complications of the metastatic melanoma.

Smokey taught me the value of leaving no stone unturned in the search for better diagnostics and therapy for a loved one stricken with cancer. This lesson will be one of Smokey's legacies. As the owner of a veterinary oncology practice, I have devoted our practice to searching for *the best* therapy available for every animal with cancer. We will ensure, to the best of our ability, to offer the best therapy available, even if that therapy is only available at another location. If I would do it for Smokey, we will do it for your pet.

The loss I felt and still feel over his death is sometimes overwhelming, but even this grief is insignificant compared to the happiness I shared with him. Whenever I feel sad, I just remember the euphoric feeling I had every time Smokey jumped into my arms as I came through my front door.

Follow the Veterinary Cancer Center
Facebook: facebook.com/vcchope/
Twitter: @VccHope
Instagram: vcchope

Spirit

INSIDE THE CANINE SOUL, PSYCHE, AND BEYOND, THE EXPERT INTERVIEWS

The bond between human and dog can be quite profound and life-changing. Dogs can be natural Spirit teachers for their loved ones, offering much-needed lessons wholly rooted in boundless love. They help us transmute the negative and bring us together. A burly firehouse dog named Duke can boost morale and alleviate stress, and a five-pound Yorkie named Chaka can help heal a family immersed in grief. They can guide us through emotional transitions and, like Angie Girl, restore a doubting heart. They might even seem to be gifts from beyond, sent by a loved one who departed long ago, like Chester, or make such an impression on us at first sight, like Cooper, Honey, or Rhodie in how they clearly and knowingly chose *us*.

They are so in tune with our hearts—and even sometimes slightly obsessed with the beat of them, like Clay! They teach us to persevere and have faith by way of example, like how Max proved he would bravely beat all odds and walk again. Sometimes our pets are clearly tapping into the unseen forces, like when Maxine "sees Spirits." Other times, they perform a critical life or death assist, like when Buster alerted his companion to a grand mal seizure about to happen while driving alone.

These inspiring stories are just a few examples of the greater, divine forces that permeate the human and dog connection and the imperceptible influences that frequently guide them. More aspects of these inherent, invisible energies are presented here in the Spirit section, which span the gamut from harnessing energy to heal using Reiki to tapping into tips from animal communicator Eileen Garfinkel to intuitively connect more. Psychic medium Kim Russo points out, "Animals instinctively understand energy, it goes back to their primitive nature. Having a very deep psychic connection with their owners, as well as their environment, helps them to naturally understand the energy tone that is being emitted in their surroundings."

Virtually every dog's family interviewed revealed how their dog regularly operates on an extrasensory level, keenly sensing happenings before they occur, knowing when a family member will be arriving home or leaving for a trip, or how so many sense when their loved ones are sick, like Izzy, Buddy, and Rookie, who will never leave their ill companions' sides.

When that heartbreaking day comes when they pass on, like our friends Daisy, Zoey, Ellie, Ginger, Boscoe, and Cookie Nutella have, Wendy Van de Poll offers compassionate tips to navigate the grieving process and help answer the tough question of when the time is right to get another pet. Van de Poll also explains how the death of a loved one—or two beloved feline friends in the case of Toby—can have a deep impact on their psyche, yet during, they can step up and courageously take on the role of emotional guardian.

One commonality for most dog owners is the reminder that they receive from their dogs about living in the present. For dogs, this is their permanent state of mind. They don't live in the past or worry about the future. Centering your awareness in the here and now may serve as one of the greatest dog-to-human spiritual gifts of all.

Sarah Hauser

Animal Reiki Expert | HealingEnergyforAnimals.com

Reiki means universal healing energy. Animal Reiki is harnessing energy that can help your dog relax, heal, and release negative behaviors, pain, toxins, or traumatic experiences. Sarah Hauser is a Reiki Master with a special certification in Animal Reiki as well as Bach Flower Remedies. She dedicates nearly all her free time to administering Reiki to stressed-out or abused animals in shelters. These compassionate, therapeutic treatments greatly enhance their well-being and adoptability. Hauser's heart is in it.

In all her years of working on animals, she has found that fear and anxiety are the root of many animals' issues. Fear and anxiety can manifest in various ways through the mind (e.g., separation anxiety), body (aggression, hiding), spirit (holding onto past traumatic events), or space (excessive digging, chewing, etc.).

"Reiki helps animals access that calm space. This will build on itself, and after time, the dog will be better able to find that space on their own," Hauser says. She uses a combination of observation and intuition, asking, "What is this dog showing me right now, and what is he or she ready to do? What will be most beneficial for them?" Sometimes she starts out by getting the dog moving with some exercises and leash work. In other circumstances, she may just sit with the dog and offer Reiki to them for the whole session. She stresses that an important concept is spending quality time with your dog—especially for people who think they are too busy for this to work. "Doing a meditation, sitting quietly with your pet, even if it's for ten minutes, twice a day, can make a huge difference," she says. Here, Sarah offers her top ways to soothe anxiety and create a deeper connection with your pet and adds, "having a connection with a dog can make us better people."

Healing Bubble Meditation

This will help you to share a quiet, loving, beautiful time and space with your dog— truly being in the moment with them.

You can do this for as little as ten minutes or as long as an hour. You can make it part of a routine with your dog, and you both will benefit from it.

Sit in a position that is comfortable for you in the presence of your dog. Wherever your dog chooses to be is fine. If you have more than one dog, they can all be present for the meditation if you wish. Take a few deep, cleansing breaths and let your body and mind quiet down. Let any worries or expectations that come up float away. Imagine a bubble of white, healing light around you—a bubble of peace and harmony. Let your dog know they are loved and safe.

Invite your dog (silently or aloud) into the bubble, letting them know they are welcome to take as much or as little of the energy as they wish. Your dog may come close to you and want some petting, or they may choose to sit farther away.

When you feel it is time to end the meditation, thank your dog for being a partner in the healing and meditation process. Continue to sit quietly for a time before getting up. Let your dog rest for a while if they wish.

Three Top Tips to Calm Your Dog

1. Compression shirts or body wraps

An anti-anxiety compression shirt can help bring a dog's stress level down whether the stress is generalized or more specific such as thunder, fireworks, loud noises, going to the vet, etc. You can find them online or at most pet stores.

A body wrap is an inexpensive alternative to a compression shirt. Purchase an ACE bandage at any drugstore. If your dog is large, you can tie two together. A two-inch bandage is good for a smaller dog, a three-inch bandage for a larger dog. Try to wrap your dog slowly, using a soothing voice and treats when needed.

2. Ear Work

Acupressure to the ear can be extremely calming. This consists of circular touches and strokes done on the ear, where there are acupressure points along the triple heater

meridian relating to the respiratory, digestive, and reproductive systems. Stroke the ear from the base of the ear all the way out to the tip to hit all points. This is easy to do when you have your dog out for a walk, are on the way to the vet, etc.

3. Bach Flower Remedies

Bach Rescue Remedy contains five different Bach Flower essences and is beneficial and safe for animals as well as for people. Rescue Remedy has a very calming effect and can be used

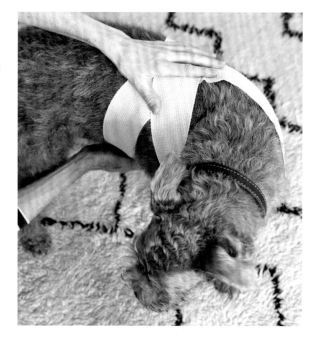

for a variety of stressful situations, as well as for general anxiety. It is often helpful to give the Rescue Remedy in both drops and spray form. The drops can be given by:

1. Putting two drops on a treat or dab of wet food;
2. Putting two drops directly in the dog's mouth with the dropper;
3. Putting a few drops on your hand and rubbing on the inside tips of the dog's ear;
4. Putting a few drops on your hand and petting your dog gently down the back, all the way down the tail, as well, if they are comfortable with that;
5. Putting a few drops on your hand and offering your hand for your dog to lick off;
6. Putting ten drops in water.

You can administer the remedy four times a day, or more often if there is a lot of anxiety and agitation. One drop of the remedy holds the energy of the essence, so frequency is more important than the amount you are giving. When the animal shows a shift in behavior, you can lessen frequency of the dosage.

A Rescue Remedy spray can be sprayed in the environment to promote a relaxed feeling. You can spray four times a day either on bedding, clothing, or where your dog experiences the most anxiety like a car or carrier. It's recommended to choose the Rescue Remedy made for animals because it uses glycerin rather than alcohol.

"It's a small thing to help one animal, but to that one animal it's a big thing." —**Gene Baur, cofounder of Farm Sanctuary**

Kim Russo

Psychic Medium, TV Personality,
Author of *The Happy Medium: Life Lessons from the Other Side*

Kim Russo is a world-renowned psychic medium, known for turning around even the most ardent cynics on her Lifetime Movie Network television shows, *The Haunting of . . .* and *Psychic Intervention,* but she herself also started out as a cynic.

She describes herself as a levelheaded, grounded, and logical person. And although she could speak to the dead since she was nine, she kept her gift under wraps for a long time. She considers herself an "ordinary" person and in her book *The Happy Medium* reveals how everyone can harness his or her intuition. "Spiritual gifts aren't granted only to special individuals who sit in the yoga position on faraway mountain tops and chant all day long. They are also given to very ordinary people like you and me," the Long Island mom says. "We can learn from animals. They do not have ego and they don't rationalize. They teach us to be in the moment." Here, Kim shares the unique way that dogs communicate and how we can better communicate with them.

Can you give an example or two of how you psychically connected to Mugsy and Maggie? Was there anything you did that helped enhance that connection? [Mugsy and Maggie were Shih Tzus who lived to the age of eighteen and recently passed.]

One day, Mugsy decided to sneak out of my backyard by squeezing under my fence. He was gone for a bit, and I was scouring the neighborhood looking for him in my car and I took Maggie along for the ride. Then it dawned on me. I decided to calm down, close my eyes, and picture him walking up to my front door. Then I mentally sent out the signal stating that he had enough time to wander and explore and now it is time to come home where he belongs. I went one step further and looked into Maggie's eyes and mentally told her to call Mugsy in her mind. Although Mugsy was the male dog, Maggie ruled the roost and kept him in check. I then decided to go straight home and wait for my little guy to hear my call. Not even five minutes from the time I arrived home did I see him strolling down the block and walk directly up to my front door. I decided to wait outside, inside of my car, until he returned safely. Some may say this can be coincidence; however, this happened with Mugsy on more occasions than I care to remember, and every time I put out the intention for him to return home, he did. I'd like to think he heard me calling.

Animals instinctively understand energy, and it goes back to their primitive nature. They have a keen sense of awareness to avoid danger in the wild, and they use all of their physical senses, such as smell, touch, and hearing, which are more highly developed in dogs. They also use their psychic senses, way more than we humans do. Having a very deep psychic connection with their owners, as well as their environment, helps them to naturally understand the energy tone that is being emitted in their surroundings. Dogs can very easily adapt to their owners' emotional vibration right from the minute the relationship begins. The one thing that I did to enhance the psychic connection between me and M & M is that I made them feel as safe and secure as possible right from the minute they came into my life. Trust is the number-one element when forming any relationship or bond, whether between two humans or between pets and humans. They quickly depended on me for their safety, love, and care, and I depended on them to give me the most unconditional love and lots of puppy kisses.

You mentioned that dogs communicate in symbols and feelings. Is it best when we are trying to communicate with dogs to also use symbols and feelings to communicate rather than "words"?

Since dogs are not able to communicate verbally, they are naturally in tune to receiving signals mind-to-mind by using telepathy. They are very visual creatures, and they can see images and pictures that we send them. For example, if I wanted them to go in their beds, I would first visualize the room where their beds were, and I would picture them walking in that room and stepping into their beds. I would follow up this vision by verbally saying, "Please go into your bed now." By sending them the picture of their bed, along with positive reinforcement by using a sweet tone, they knew this was not a punishment, but rather a loving request. More often than not, dogs will want to please their owners, who have been caring for and loving to them.

"The Rainbow Bridge" for pets [when they cross over] has become as psychically ubiquitous and acknowledged as the Akashic records are to departed humans. Have you ever had any impressions or visuals of this canine rite of passage to the other side?

As a psychic medium, I have communicated with thousands of departed souls over the years. There has been numerous times in which a soul will step forward with their departed pets. I have seen animals ranging from birds, cats, dogs, horses, elephants, and even kangaroos. Like on earth, where animals coexist with humans, it is the same beyond the veil. On the other side, there is an animal kingdom that coexists and comingles with the human kingdom. The only difference there is that you will see animals who lived in the wild here on earth coexist with humans without the need for precaution. The only reason an animal here on earth is ever a danger to society is that it is necessary for him to hunt his prey for food. Since we do not take the physical body with us, there is no need to eat or for food. Therefore, the love that the animals naturally express to one another here in nature can be expressed to other kingdoms on the other side. When conducting a reading, I often see pets running in green open fields or prancing around in large meadows with many vivid colors of trees and flowers that cannot be described in human terms. The best way to describe it is how The Land of Oz automatically turned from black and white to brilliant shades of color as Dorothy went on her journey; and as it is with Dorothy, we all will wind up "Somewhere over the Rainbow," including our beloved canine companions.

In many of the interviews I'm doing with dog owners, I am often hearing, "My dog knows when I'm sick and won't leave my side." Or "My dog knows when I'm sad." Why do you think this is so common, and what exactly do you think

they are picking up on? Is it an energetic connection they feel, or is it a lack of movement and change of routine?

I believe the answer is both. Although Mugsy and Maggie understood words I spoke to them verbally, most often our psychic connections were based on a telepathic level. This is how dogs can naturally connect with other animals' thoughts, feelings, needs, or wants. As many animals travel in packs, it is their innate response to take care of their own and to be loyal to those who are in the pack. It is the basic survival skill for any species. There is power in numbers who stick together. Dogs will consider a person to be part of their pack and can sense what humans need. The communication between Mugsy, Maggie, and myself was on a deeper level. We used a higher-energy vibration that went beyond using verbal words. Contained in these vibrations are variations of emotions. We all understood and sensed a tone or vibration of each other's moods and actions. They knew when I was happy or sad, and they knew what I needed, and vice versa. Dogs can hear frequencies beyond the capability of a human, and they can smell things such as illness. Although they can't tell us, they also feel emotions of others on a very deep level. This has been proven to me over and over throughout the course of the eighteen years that we had together. I considered them my fur babies, and just like a mother knows what their child needs without them verbally stating it, so it was with us.

Follow Kim
Twitter: @TheHappyMedium
Instagram: KimRussoMedium
Facebook: https://www.facebook.com/kimthehappymedium/

Eileen Garfinkel

Animal Communicator | DreamsofAmelia.com

Eileen Garfinkel communicates with dogs by hearing words, seeing symbolic pictures, and receiving certain feelings and emotions. After a session, she doesn't remember much of what she has said but does recall that most messages are about "needing more exercise" and a soul-to-soul message rather than the mundane declarations of "I don't like that red bowl!" She says that one of her biggest tips for making a dog happy is to "give your dog a job which lends them a feeling of accomplishment. They like to discover, to hunt, and to figure out." You can count on Eileen to pick up very specific information that only you and your dog would know.

Do people mainly seek your services for behavioral issues with their dogs? And if so, what are the main reasons why dogs are "misbehaving"?

I'd say 50 percent of my clients are seeking answers to behavioral issues. Forty percent want to know what is going on medically or physically with their dogs—although I am quick to say that I am not a veterinarian and whatever I may intuit must be checked with a medical professional. And the last 10 percent want to make sure their dogs are happy and wonder if any changes need to be made to ensure their dogs' happiness.

There are myriad reasons why dogs "misbehave." What we see as inappropriate behavior is perfectly appropriate to them. A dog doesn't rip through the trash or tear up the rug for no reason. It's not because he or she is "bad." The dog is trying to convey a message to its guardian. Maybe it's "I'm bored" or "I need more exercise" or "The dog walker only walks for ten minutes instead of the hour you're paying for!" Whatever it is, it's an appropriate response for the dog, however inappropriate to the human. It has been my experience that "misbehavior" is a reaction to the relationship and/or the environment.

You've said the animals pick up on our energy and read our intentions. Does that mean that when we are anxious or happy, they immediately feel that way, too?

Dogs are social animals. They read our faces, our body language, and the sound and tone of our voices. But more than that, dogs are without ego; therefore, their intuition is purer than we can imagine. I like to say that dogs are pure spirit. They see our hearts. Some may mirror our own emotions and, for example, feel the anxiety we are feeling. In that way, they are our teachers. We can see ourselves through their eyes. Others may feel our anxiety, and because of who they are, they may begin to "mother" us, trying to comfort us. Others take on protective roles and seemingly become "aggressive," trying to protect us from the world. Every dog, just like every human, is an individual, and every relationship is unique. It seems to me that we all get the dog we are supposed to have for our soul's betterment, whether or not we consciously know that. Furthermore, every dog, like every human, has a path and a journey particular to that individual.

Why do so many dogs get upset when their loved ones yell? They scurry away and leave the room, even if they are neutrally speaking up so someone else can hear them?

Haha! My dog runs into the bedroom every time I use talk and text [cellular voice command]. Dogs are wholly sensitive to their environment. As domesticated as they are, they are still dogs, not humans! Every nuance in their environment is noted, although most are not acted upon. Watch your dog's nose twitch as soon as the door opens. Some experts estimate that your dog can detect smells 10,000 to 100,000 times better than we can. Imagine that! And their hearing is at least four times greater than ours. So that is the physical answer to why they get upset when we raise our voices. The other reason a dog chooses to leave the room when we raise our voices is that they are sensitive to the tones and nuances we use. Why are you raising your voice? The difference in the sound may startle them or even confuse them. Why are you being so loud? There are dogs that don't do more than lift an ear when we are loud. Some of the difference in behavior may have to do with how the dog was raised (rescue, pet shop, breeder, multihomes, abuse, etc.), and some has to do with genetics.

Do dogs worry? Do they have the same gamut of human emotions that we do? I know you've mentioned they don't feel regret. What other general human emotion do they not feel?

Worry is about anticipating an event that hasn't happened yet. Because dogs live in the moment, worry isn't part of the gamut of emotions that they feel. They neither anticipate the future nor regret the past. As we all do, dogs register memories in the cells of their bodies. That's why a dog who has been abused might cower when you try to pet him. It's not that he's saying, "Uh oh, I'm worried that a punch is coming." But he is reacting to what he has learned in the past. A person standing above him is a reminder of what happened in the past when a person stood above him and hit him. Dogs have memories, but they don't have worries. They don't say, "Gee, I wish that never happened to me and now it's happening again." But they do feel, "I know that stance. It means pain."

Often, people ask me to tell their dogs that the family will be moving to a new house. It's not possible to convey that message in that way. Dogs don't project into the future. They truly live in the present. However, doing something like walking the dog in the new neighborhood, visiting the new house with the dog (if possible), and when moving in, bringing lots of things from the old house that the dog knows—a favorite blanket, bones, toys, etc.—will help him/her to adapt. Using Bach Flower Essences or other essences that deal with change and adapting to new circumstances can be of great benefit.

As for other human emotions that they don't feel, they don't feel anything that has to do with ego. For example—and this is only an example—every dog is different, and there are many reasons a dog barks or growls, but if a dog growls at another dog, he is not feeling "superior" or "tough" or "I'm gonna show him who's boss!" He may be reacting to a scent, an energy, a stance. He may be feeling territorial, protective, or insecure. A dog that is insecure will want to protect his area, his yard, his food, his toys, etc. Or he may be feeling fearful. He may be picking up an anxious energy from his guardian and feel the need to protect. Dogs don't feel embarrassed, humiliated, haughty, conceited, grandiose, or self-righteous. Any ego-based feelings are foreign to dogs.

What has been the most surprising communication that has ever come through in a reading?

There have been so many surprises over the years! I remember a little Chihuahua named Bobo who had recently been adopted from a shelter. During my initial connection with him, he told me that he wanted to be called Bennie. When I spoke to his guardian, I asked him if he was thinking of changing Bobo's name to Bennie, and he said that his partner had woken up that morning singing Elton John's "Bennie and the Jets." Did Bobo pick up the thought from his guardian, or did the guardian pick up the thought from Bobo? I believe that we are all connected. I don't think it really matters!

Another time, a client was wondering if she should get a second dog. I connected with the resident dog, who told me to tell his guardians that he did not want "Freddy." When I told the human client, she said she had just come from a party where the host had an out-of-control dog who was jumping on everyone and everything. His name was Freddy! The guardian asked me to tell the resident dog that she would not bring home anyone who was like Freddy!

And another amazing session happened with a little Japanese Chin whose primary caregiver had died tragically and unexpectedly. This little dog had stopped eating, didn't want to go out, was listless and uninterested in everything. Her other guardian reached out to me, and when I connected with Kiko, instead of hearing a grief-stricken lament, I heard what sounded like a petulant, spoiled child! She told me that she was used to be carried and hand-fed. She just did not approve at all of the way life had turned out for her! I was floored! I reminded Kiko of what it was like to be a dog, reminded her that she chose to come into this life in a dog body and what a pity if she didn't take advantage of it. I showed her what it was like to be dog—running and playing, stealing food from her dog siblings, getting the best spot on the couch, running free in the dog park. I spent about thirty minutes psychically getting into a dog's body and feeling the joy of being a dog. I shared all of that with her, and, according to her guardian, she had an immediate turnaround and became a sassy and playful dog, enjoying all the wonderful things dogs enjoy.

And then there are the surprisingly sad communications, such as the dog who wanted to be rehomed. He was unhappy where he was. He was not able to get the exercise he needed, nor was he given much one-on-one time. It was difficult because the person loved him. He was eventually rehomed. Love does what's best for the other.

Have you ever not been able to connect to a pet?

There was one time I couldn't connect. When I tried to connect, it felt like I was coming up against a wall and the only thing I could hear was the dog telling me that she didn't want medication. I had no idea why she was saying that. When I talked to her guardian, the woman told me she had her dog on Prozac and she was not going to stop the medication. Interesting . . . However, I have had communications with other animals on those kinds of drugs and was able to connect. I never suggest ceasing a drug without medical intervention. I may suggest holistic or behavioral alternatives, but whatever I suggest must always be checked out with a medical professional. I often give my clients the names of holistic veterinarians.

In your readings, you seem to really pick up on the love that the dog has for their human. Have you ever picked up otherwise?

I have never felt anything from the dog to the human other than love. We say that dogs give us unconditional love, and they do. As I previously related, I have known dogs who needed rehoming, but it was not because the dogs didn't love the their guardians. There are always soul lessons. Giving the dog away was a great lesson about love and letting go for one person. It was a lesson in self-sacrifice for the greater good. It was doing what was right for the other.

Are dogs also psychic? If there was an unhealthy issue for them, would they know why? Let's say a dog was suffering from allergies. Is it common to hear them say, "Hey, I'm allergic to the chicken I'm eating!"

To psychically connect with animals means that the animals and the humans involved send and receive information in ways that both can understand. Our spirits naturally understand the energy or vibration of every word or image that is projected. The intention, energy, or vibration is translated in ways the human and the animal can understand. It's like having an instant translator in your brain. So, yes, dogs are psychic. But does the dog tell me he's allergic to chicken? Sometimes, yes. Sometimes I receive information from the dog's spirit guides, my spirit guides, or other high beings. Often, I don't know where the information is coming from. It pours in, and I am there to receive it. Many times I will connect with a dog and feel a pain in my hip or leg. Or I suddenly feel nauseated. I am picking up the pain or ailment from the dog. Is the dog telling me about his pain? Again, I refer to the connectedness of all life. We are all made up of energies that go beyond the physical. Our energy doesn't end where our bodies end but go far beyond into the universe that surrounds us. When I am able to get on the dog's frequency, I am able to pick up information.

Throughout *The Holistic Dog*, so many families have said that their dog came to them in a "meant to be" way. Why is it that the dogs in our lives offer such divine connection and life lessons?

Everything in our lives can be life lessons or soul lessons if we choose to look at life in that way. Depending on one's idea of the Divine, we can learn from anything that comes into our lives. I believe that we come into one another's lives to enrich our soul's journeys in order to evolve. Not all of us choose to do or see that. And that's fine. There is no judgment in love. And choosing not to see or learn is, in truth, part of our journey!

I believe that when we feel our dogs were "meant to be" part of our lives, we are right. Perhaps we have "soul contracts" among our friends, family, and animals before we incarnated into this life. Perhaps we have lived lives before this present life—reincarnation. Perhaps we need to balance what happened to us in other lives—karma. This is the mystery of synchronicity, if you will. I believe that dogs and all animals are nearer to the Divine that most people and, in that way, they can teach us life lessons in a way that humans cannot. As I said previously, they have no ego. They are not in our lives to dominate the land, acquire money, steal our wealth, or wield power over people. They are dogs. They are instinctual and intuitive. They see the intentions behind our words and our behaviors. It's easy to see why they are able to teach us life lessons. It's easy to feel that they are meant to be in our lives.

The story of how I adopted my own dog, Tootsie, is a case in point. I began walking a friend's dog about five years ago, more as a favor than a job, but about a year into it, my friend told her new neighbor about me. The woman had recently moved to our neighborhood from another state and was looking for a dog walker. When she called and told me about her dog, my heart filled with love. I had never seen her dog, didn't know anything about her, not even what she looked like, but I knew that I loved her. I met Tootsie a day or two later, and I felt an instant bond. People who knew me would tell me that I should get a dog because I was so good with dogs. (I'd had cats all my adult life). My answer was always, "The only dog I would ever want is Tootsie." About eight months later, Tootsie's guardian called me. Due to unforeseen circumstances, she could no longer keep Tootsie and asked if I would adopt her. She said I was the only person she would trust to care for Tootsie as much as she did! That was over three years ago, and I've always felt that her previous guardian, who saved Tootsie from terrible abuse, was the conduit to bring Tootsie into my life. That is not to say that Tootsie didn't belong where she was previously. She certainly did! But her journey brought her to me, where she will stay the rest of her life.

How can anyone communicate telepathically with their dog? Do you recommend any exercises to hone this unspoken communication?
It is my belief that all humans have telepathic abilities. Some refer to this ability as intuition, others as psychic ability or sixth sense. Whether we realize it or not, we are always communicating nonverbally. Did you ever walk into a room and instantly dislike or like a person you've never met before? Have you experienced thinking about a person you haven't seen or spoken with in months and you unexpectedly run into that person on the street? That is a nonverbal communication. Animal communication is the ability to allow Universal Mind or Energy to express itself through us. Because it is the same energy that moves through everything everywhere, once we practice tapping into that energy, we can communicate with all of life. Meditation is a great way to begin to calm your mind enough to begin hearing/seeing/sensing other energies.

In my experience, most guardians are already communicating with their dogs! For example, I might tell a guardian that her dog is longing for her ex-husband and the guardian will say, "I knew that! I thought so!!"

Here are some very basic steps to begin communicating with your dog:

1. Find your calm center. Slow down. Pay attention to your breathing. Slowly breathe in and out in an easy, relaxed manner. Relax your body and focus on the breath. You can also use meditation or relaxation exercises or CDs to help bring your mind into a relaxed, receptive state.

2. Connect by bringing Universal Energy in through the crown of your head and allowing it to circulate throughout your body.

3. Ground yourself in Mother Earth by visualizing energy running down your spine through your body into the Earth.

4. Invite your dog to get quiet with you. Your dog doesn't have to be in the same room with you or even in the same country! He or she may be in your presence, or you can use a photo if the animal is in another location, or just imagine the animal in your mind.

5. Connect to him or her by asking if s/he is ready to communicate or wants to communicate with you at this time.

6. Open your heart or your Third Eye chakra. Allow yourself to experience the fundamental nature of your dog, his or her true essence. Imagine a river of light or a laser beam or a golden funnel from your heart or Third Eye chakra to your dog's heart or Third Eye chakra.

7. Ask questions. Think the thought clearly and project that thought to the animal, visualizing the thought as a picture or simply sending the words and believing the animal will receive the intention behind the words. You can project the thought and send it along via the techniques in step 6.

8. Listen and believe what you receive. You may receive the answers in one or any combination of the methods—emotions, scents, pictures, words, feelings, etc. Acknowledge the answers.

9. Thank your dog.

The biggest obstacle to communicating with animals is our own skepticism, our own inner critic. Not believing that what you are receiving is real is one of the most common blocks to telepathic animal communication.

One of the greatest returns to learning to communicate with our dogs is that we begin to understand that we can communicate with all of life. When we communicate with animals, we connect to Spirit, and we are given the opportunity to rediscover a way of relating that goes beyond what we can see. We reawaken the mystery, the majesty, and the magic that is Life. It is truly a journey worth taking.

Wendy Van de Poll, MS, CEOL

Certified End-of-Life and Pet Loss Grief Coach | CenterForPetLossGrief.com

Wendy Van de Poll is a pioneering leader in the field of pet loss grief support and the founder of the Center for Pet Loss Grief. She has written the best-selling books *My Dog Is Dying: What Do I Do?*, *My Dog Has Died: What Do I Do? The Pet Bereavement Series* and *Healing A Child's Pet Loss Grief: A Guide for Parents*. She provides wisdom, joy, and compassion for grief relief in her practice. Wendy is a certified end-of-life and grief coach, pet funeral celebrant, and a licensed massage therapist for humans, horses, and hounds.

Did you begin this vocational path and start the Center for Pet Loss Grief because of your own experience losing Marley?

When Marley was diagnosed with nasosarcoma, I was crushed. I was losing my best friend, confidant, life partner, and business associate (she helped me with my clients).

I tried to find help for myself, and there was nothing available of quality or depth that represented the life I had with Marley. Losing Marley was ultimately what inspired me to refocus the work that I do for animals and their people. For more than sixteen years, I was a massage therapist for humans, horses, and hounds. My animal practice by default was based in pet hospice. People would call me wanting do to something special for their companion at the end of their life. I didn't advertise this, yet the universe offered me this very tender and special avocation.

My work grew in this field, and as a pioneer, I offered many animals peaceful deaths. While I was giving massages, people would express their grief. I would quietly listen and hear the pain they were experiencing as they expressed the chaos and complexity of their journeys. It seemed as though I were being guided to help and translate the power of death and how this experience can actually give way to life for these people. That is when I studied to become a certified end-of-life and pet loss grief coach and opened the Center for Pet Loss Grief, which offers complete and intuitive heart-based support for people who are either losing a pet, dealing with the previous death of a pet, or need animal mediumship services for those who would like to know more about their pet in the afterlife.

Are the steps of grief that most humans go through in losing a loved one the same when they lose a pet? (Shock or Disbelief, Denial, Anger, Bargaining, Guilt, Depression, and Acceptance and Hope.)
Yes, the stages of grief are the same when losing a human loved one and a pet. However, in my experience, the death of a companion animal is usually more intense. Our dogs give us unconditional love, and when we lose that everyday physical reminder of how wonderful we are, it is easy for our lives to become chaotic and empty. Unconditional love is what our dogs excel in. Yes, we love our human family and friends, and they love us. Yet, is it without expectation? Probably not. So the impact and grief of losing a dog is usually greater than when a friend or family member dies.

I teach my clients that grief has a life of its own, and embracing the seven stages of grief can be extremely helpful when coping and healing the grief journey. Yet, grief is not about following a prescribed list. Grief is tenacious and can dig deep into the heart. It affects daily routines and can leave someone feeling very hopeless. The seven stages of grief are extremely valuable; the order in which people experience them is truly up to them. It is important to let them unfold naturally.

When someone you know experiences the loss of their dog, what is the best thing you can say or do for them? What should you avoid saying?
The best thing a person can do for someone when they are experiencing grief is to be there for them as a listening ear. Don't avoid them or the subject. Provide a safe environment to express themselves. This is not easy for people to do because, as a society, we have gotten very distant from the dying process. We view death as something to be afraid of and avoided.

It can be difficult to know what to say at the right time, and we can find ourselves bumbling for words. If you know someone who has lost their dog, the best thing to do is prepare yourself ahead of time to become aware of unintentional yet potential hurtful comments.

Here is a list of statements to avoid saying to someone whose dog has been diagnosed with a terminal disease or has died. I go into these statements more in my books, but you can get a general idea here.

1. It's only a dog—you can get another.
2. You are *still* grieving?
3. Let me tell you what I did after my dog died . . .

Being there as a thoughtful and compassionate friend will mean so much to the person grieving the loss of their dog. Offering unconditional love is paramount.

What do you find brings the most comfort to dog owners who are grieving?
A couple things: If the person is spiritual in nature and believes in the afterlife, getting intuitive messages from their pet really helps. So many of my clients feel guilty they didn't

do enough for their dogs. And they want to apologize and tell their dogs that they love them. Even though it may not be of physical nature, they can continue on a spiritual level to have a lifetime of connection with their dogs. Our dogs become parts of our souls, parts of our hearts. This soul connection never goes away, even at the end of life.

The other is when people begin to recognize that what they are feeling and experiencing is normal. There are so many unexpected emotions and levels of pet loss grief. Once my clients learn that and recognize what they are going through is perfectly normal, it helps make their journey feel more supported.

After the death of a pet, do you recommend getting a new pet right away?
This can be an excruciating decision and one that people are never 100 percent confident about when loss is new. For some of my clients, opening their hearts to a new dog right after their companion dies is extremely helpful. Yet for other clients, it can take a long time before they are ready. For others, they never are able to have another dog because the pain is so intense. Because the way grief is processed is unique for everyone, making the decision to get another dog is a personal choice.

Here are some things to keep in mind that I share with my clients and talk about in more detail in my books.

1. No matter where you are with your grief, the action of bringing another dog into your life can trigger feelings of loss that you thought you had already dealt with.
2. There is no right or wrong time to bring another dog into your life. It is up to you.
3. Give yourself time to grieve and think. Don't give into the pressure of others or make a hasty decision.

What, if anything, can you do while your dog is still living to prepare for their loss?
There are many things people can do while their dog is still living and healthy. I find that when people prepare for the end of the life, it can be a less chaotic. This is not

to say people won't feel grief and be devastated, but the more one prepares for them not being physically with them, the more they can have complete focus on their dog when they need their person the most. I encourage people to make lists, as lists keep anxiety and feelings of grief in check. They allow you to focus on the tasks at hand of taking care of your dog during their final days, hours, and months.

Checklists are great for creating goals and staying on task. They help people move through the day with their dog with more love and less chaos. It is easy to forget things, be disorganized, and not be prepared for important decisions and events that will occur. A checklist will help with making decisions, choosing veterinarians, and being the best advocate they can be for their dogs.

What do you recommend to do to get you through a crushing loss of a beloved pet?
I recommend self-care for clients. Massage, support groups, healthy eating, and finding safe and supportive friends. All these activities will help the body, mind, and spirit as they walk this journey. I always encourage my clients to take this grief experience by the hand and give it the love and courage it needs. Be kind and limit expectations of yourself. Be careful of what you take in from people around you. People not experiencing pet loss are going to want to fix things and make life better, which will create another reaction of grief. It takes work to cope with the loss of a beloved dog. Grief unfortunately doesn't magically go away. It has a way of hiding and encouraging people to forget. Yet, it can resurface, most times unexpectedly, so being prepared and learning everything one can about what their journey is will help.

What do you recommend if there is a lot of guilt involved with the passing of a pet, such as "I could have done more" or "If only I was more diligent with his health care" or anger (at the vet, or if another person was responsible for their death)?
Guilt is one of the most common and normal feelings of grief surrounding the death of a pet. Guilt is a tenacious emotion that can get in the way of a person's healing and also surface when a person least expects it. Generally, I recommend self-compassion for this emotion. As humans who love our dogs, we can really beat ourselves up for not

having done better. When people work with me before their dog dies, I support them by encouraging them to be as prepared as they can by picking a health-care team that is in their best interest. Having a professional team that respects their decision and wishes helps keep guilt at a minimum. However, if this is not obtainable or their dog has already died, I continue to encourage people to be kindhearted with themselves and discover ways in which they feel good about the care they did give their dogs.

I remind my clients that it takes work to heal guilt and to feel comfortable with the fact that healing will take time. Their dogs were really special, and it is important to allow emotions to happen and to experience them. Feelings of grief will not go away on their own. It takes work—and that is okay.

Do pets grieve when they lose a human family member? What about when they lose a close canine friend?

Yes, pets do grieve when they lose a human family member, and I have helped service, therapy, and family dogs that have experienced grief. It can be a very confusing time for a dog when their person dies, goes away to college, or experiences separation in a divorce situation. It is important for us to recognize and provide a healthy transition for our dogs when this happens. I have found it helpful to encourage my clients to have a verbal one-on-one conversation with them. This gives them the chance to explain to them what happened.

When a canine friend dies, they experience loss and do grieve. They can become lethargic, solitary, and not want to eat. Dogs build deep bonds with other animals, especially with their doggy friends. Since dogs are pack animals, they thrive when they experience life with another canine. Their canine friends become part of their routine and life force. They depend on their canine friends for play, companionship, and support for various situations in their lives.

Do you believe our pets tell us when they are near or ready to pass on?

Yes, I do believe dogs know when they are ready to die. This is a very important thing to be ready for by recognizing the unique signs a dog will give their owner. I prepare my clients for this moment. It can be a very difficult time, especially when faced with the question "When do I know the time is right to euthanize my dog?" Our dogs are always communicating to us through their body language and deep soul-heart connection. When we learn to listen to them, they will tell us. When clients ask me this question, I say to them, "Your dog will tell you. They will give a look, gesture, sound, that will hit you deep in the pit of your stomach or the core of your heart."

Can you share one of your favorite stories about pet grief support?

One of my favorite stories is when I was helping a client discover the positive and restorative rewards of writing a love letter to her dog, Freddy. Karen discovered that her grief was starting to affect her life to the point of not being able to go to work or talk with friends. She was really stressed that she didn't have a special way to express her love for Freddy. Karen didn't like to write; however, as we continued to work together, I encouraged her to make lists of all her lovely memories of Freddy. Then, a beautiful change happened as she began to create her lists. She discovered that she had forgotten some experiences that she'd had with Freddy, and by writing, she recalled and recaptured the amazing life she'd had with him.

When she finished her lists, she then wrote her love letter to Freddy and read it to him at his gravesite. Karen was so excited, because after she read the letter to Freddy, it increased her understanding of how Freddy helped her be a better person. It also helped her express her grief but recapture how much they meant to each other. Karen was so happy to celebrate the life she had with Freddy in this way because she learned more about herself through Freddy. It was a powerful and healing declaration of her growth and a processing of her grief in a very healthy way.

Follow Wendy
https://www.facebook.com/centerforpetlossgrief
Twitter: @CtrPetLossGrief

About the Author

Laura Benko has created the progressive lifestyle concept of connecting mind, body, spirit, and space all together. She has written *The Holistic Home: Feng Shui for Mind, Body, Spirit, Space* (Helios/Skyhorse) and is a keynote speaker, television segment host, lecturer at Pratt Institute, and the founder and CEO of The Holistic Home Company.

Follow Laura
LauraBenko.com
TheHolisticHomeCompany.com
Twitter.com/BenkoFengShui
Twitter.com/HolisticHomeCo
Instagram.com/TheHolisticHomeCompany
Facebook.com/TheHolisticHomeCompany

Interview with the Author

by her sister, Lisa Benko-Rodriguez

Laura Benko

www.LauraBenko.com

As your older sister, I've watched you evolve into an expert in your field of Feng Shui and take it to a whole new level, writing *The Holistic Home*, now *The Holistic Dog*, and also start and grow a successful business—all within a very short time. To witness all of these amazing milestones in your life has brought me such great joy. I'm honored to interview you and share your insights into the Mind, Body, Spirit, and Space connection. So, what made you go from writing *The Holistic Home* to writing *The Holistic Dog*?

In talking to Susan—who took the beautiful cover photo of *The Holistic Home* and several other photographs for that book, she mentioned "a dog-in-their-home" kind of book to do together. We wanted a combination of a coffee table type of book to showcase the dogs in their spaces, along with a practical resource that delved into the canine mind, body and spirit. It felt like a natural evolution in my holistic lifestyle concepts I created and teach that deeply examine the connection of mind, body, spirit and space all together.

You documented the stories of many different dogs in your book. Which story stood out the most to you? Was there a particular dog that tugged on your heartstrings?

So many of these dogs' stories touched me in many different ways. However, while doing the interview with Simba, I was overcome with emotion witnessing Simba's utter devotion to guide and protect his companion every single minute. He was keenly aware that he was working and was constantly looking at his companion to not only gauge what was needed, but to anticipate what may come. This within itself is somewhat against the innate canine nature of "living in the moment," not to mention just an extraordinary feat on its own. I was moved to tears to see their connection. Then, I was moved to fury to hear how she is *still* turned away from clueless businesses that don't know that it is against the law to do so. I also learned how terribly disruptive it is to even *pet* Seeing Eye® dogs when they are resting. Doing so could create a dynamic where they start to seek out affection from strangers, which can be extremely problematic to their companions.

What have been the biggest surprises that you've discovered while researching canine health and interviewing experts for this book?

The biggest eye-opener for me was the health ramifications of overvaccinating. Until very recently, vets were going on the schedule recommended by the pharmaceutical companies that make and profit from the vaccinations, which is absurd. Vaccinations are also a big part of many vets' income, so I get how this is a heated topic. It comes down to educating yourself, doing titers, never vaccinating a sick or immune compromised pet, and, if needed, having the dosage adjusted for size and weight.

Laura and Lisa's Shetland Sheepdog, Rusty, lived to 19.5 years old.

Your Spirit section—as well as several of the dogs' stories here—delves into how dogs come into our life for a reason. We were lucky to have our beloved Sheltie, Rusty, growing up. Now, you have Yogi, and I have *The Holistic Dog* cover girl, Sunny— who, by the way, love each other very much. Watching them run side by side like two Clydesdale horses when

they're together always puts a smile on my face. What have you learned from Rusty and Yogi?

Growing up with Rusty was the greatest gift. He was a part of all our childhood moments. Like many other families' stories in this book, as kids we learned about responsibility through caring for him, and we learned about the unconditional love that a dog gives. With Yogi, I learned what has also become a popular theme of the book. Dogs live in the moment, and they help you do the same. The gift of being present is priceless.

You are the Founder and CEO of The Holistic Home Company. I've enjoyed watching your company go through some extraordinary growth in the past couple of years. You make high-quality products for the mind, body, spirit, and space. I don't think I could live without your Skin & Spirit Sensual massage oil and the Anti-Aging and Joy beauty serum. My skin just drinks it in! The crystal napkin rings always leave my dinner guests in awe of their beauty—I display them even when I'm not using them. I love how you're always adding to your product line. While writing this book, you developed a line of all-natural dog products. What inspired you to do that?

Thanks for the endorsement, Lisa. Might I add, your skin is looking supple, glowing, and radiant! I started *The Holistic Dog* product division because Yogi was suffering from bad allergies. Rounds of conventional antibiotics made it worse. The soothing bath soak I made by grinding up organic chamomile buds, organic oatmeal, and Epsom salts was the only treatment that helped him. He's also a sensitive fella that can get freaked out by loud noises and leaves the room when voices are raised. The Calm spray helped him chill out. I spray it on his bed, too. After much research and development, we rolled out a line that dogs—and their owners—love.

Are you still personally writing thank-you notes with every order?

I sure do. The only exception is when we are in the midst of our fourth quarter—our busiest time—and my director of operations, Desirée Guédez, will write some. I am grateful for every order and hope to continue this custom. Not only are all the products made while holding a positive intention, but it's also what the company culture is based on, and I will continue to strive to uphold that.

You've written *The Holistic Home* and *The Holistic Dog*. Now what?

Well, I've been thinking about this, and I'd really love to write the third book in this series with you! You are such a natural, intuitive medicine woman, have so much knowledge about holistic health, and have been integral to my own healing journey. You are also a born writer. I'd love to coauthor *Holistic You: A Healing and Wellness Guide for the Mind, Body, Spirit, Space.* What do you say, sister Sassy?

I would be honored. Thank you, sister.

About the Photographer

Known by her clients for "great range, impeccable lighting, and a strong eye for composition," Susan Fisher Plotner is an accomplished photographer who highlights the talents and achievements of award-winning architects, designers, and others in the business of building and design. She loves that her work is as varied as our built environment and takes great pleasure in photographing the perfect, simple design of a

Credit: A. Fryxell Photography. www.afryxellphotography.com

kitchen bowl *and* the powerful architecture of a flood barrier. She is based in New York and London and is a regular contributor to the *New York Times*. For a virtual stroll through our diverse, vibrant, and constantly delighting design environment, go to Susan's website, follow her on social media, get in contact. Susan welcomes new commissions, large or small, here or there—all are visually intriguing!

Follow Susan
SusanFisherPhoto.com
Houzz: Susan Fisher Photography
Instagram.com/susanfisherphoto
Twitter.com/susanfphoto
Facebook.com/SusanFisherPhoto

Interview with the Photographer

Susan Fisher Plotner

Photographer, *The Holistic Dog: Inside the Canine Mind, Body, Spirit, Space* |
www.SusanFisherPhoto.com

Susan, you have gone into the homes of 108 dogs to capture their portraits. Surely, you must have some interesting stories. Can we play a word association game? What comes to mind for the following:

Biggest dog? Monty Doodle Doo—just a huge presence! On his hind legs, he certainly seemed taller than my sons, who are six-foot-two and six-foot-three!

Most chaotic shoot? The most chaotic or simply the most challenging shoots were those involving dogs that move. HA! Remember, my usual work is photographing architecture and interiors—very static. Actually, some dogs were excellent posers (Jock, Dawkey, Charlie Ryan), while others were just nonstop action. Codega comes to mind—boundless puppy energy in a very large body, made it difficult to catch all of him in a frame! Then there were Rex and Jem—darlings both, but neither liked the actual physical camera and made every effort to render themselves invisible so that the big scary thing did not follow them around.

Most challenging work conditions? Photographing Baci and Pesto in 102-degree Atlanta August sunshine. Literally the only thing to do to stay cool, calm, and focused (pun intended!) was to get into the pool, fully clothed.

Hardest dog to photograph? Five dogs at once—Davey, Ruby, Molly, Norma, and Toro! Four dogs at once—Truman, Poppy, Stella, and Venus!

Sweetest dog? Oh, this is too difficult. Chanel—in a "big galumph" sort of way. Rugby—in an "I'm a groovy puppy with a crazy hairdo" sort of way. Chester—in an "I totally love my mom" sort of way.

Saddest shoot? Daisy. But even though very sad (Daisy would be put down the next day), it was a profoundly touching experience shared with a dear friend. I love that Daisy had a bit of cream cheese on her whiskers, which was the only food she was eating at the end.

Funniest shoot? Watching Winnie play with water in a soaking wet-turned-muddy backyard and then being allowed to relax in the middle of her "mother's" bed on the white bedspread! And Rhodie—she actually dances!

Favorite picture? Besides any and all photographs of Rosie? ;-) Well, I would have to give a shout-out to Cookie Nutella, who, thanks to a very talented design client, was the germ of this idea, and Ace, the other seedling, who quietly watched from his chair as I photographed his home.

Most unexpected event that occurred on a shoot? Being bitten! And another unexpected event was witnessing Buster help his "mother" clean up her closet and put away her shoes, literally!

Most inspiring dog? Cooper, the black lab mix with three legs. But perhaps more inspiring are his "parents," who adopted Cooper despite him being less than perfect. I love this about them.

You traveled throughout the United States, as well as internationally, for this book. Out of all the spaces you've been in, which ones were the most memorable? Photographing Aries amidst the black raspberry bushes on a Vermont hillside was a definite high point. And Thor camouflaged in the autumn leaves was another visual treat. And then there was the "stuff" of my regular job: stunning interiors; the homes of Atticus and Sunny come to mind. But perhaps my favorite image of *space* is that of tiny Chaka in front of huge doors. Made for the camera!

I know it's hard to pick a favorite dog. But a few must stand out to you. Which ones made the deepest impression on you and why? Too difficult. I love the dogs that are boundless in their dogginess: Shane, Monty, and Enzo, Dexter. And I love the dogs that have a serene bond with their humans: Sonya, Sedona, Duke. I love the "minis": Honey, Angie, Muppet. And the "maxis": Mulligan, Moose, and Ginger, Zero. Sorry, love 'em all. (Of course, Rosie is my #1!)

What would you say was the most unexpected lesson you learned by doing this project? I get my eye from my dad and an extensive paternal lineage of artists, architects, and engineers. From my mom (and her father), I get my bighearted love of dogs and our living world. Of course, I am fully aware of my DNA, yet a delightful element of this project was bringing the two parts of me together!

Most of the dog owners were present during the shoot. Did you ever witness any special connection between the dogs and their humans that you found remarkable?
I think I remarked to you somewhere along the journey that I found the photo shoots to be as much about the human as about the dog. Each and every shoot was a very personal dog-human experience, and this totally "sealed the deal" for me in terms of the significance of our book.

When shooting the experts, did anything surprising happen?
The English have a wonderful word for being surprised: *gobsmacked*! I was gobsmacked to witness Yogi literally fall into a state of sublime relaxation under the hands of Reiki expert Sarah Hauser. Even with a large camera in front of him! Remarkable.

I've been with you when you were shooting in very challenging conditions, like the fluorescent-lit, crowded, tiny examination room of Dr. Marty Goldstein; wrangling Maxine on a hot balcony; and the confines of how and where Simba had to be shot. Yet, you still rocked it and delivered perfect photographs. Do you know the exact moment when you capture that winning photo?
Actually yes. I often know the moment I have *the* image. It happens more often than not on a shoot. And bizarrely, it is generally either the very first image or the very last!

Please share with us your favorite dog story.
I love how you have brought my images to life with your stories, Laura. Who would know that Max is a medical miracle? Or what the life of Seeing Eye® Simba is like on a day-to-day basis? Or that Lou Lou likes a back massage, Clay likes to go to work, and Zuzu enjoys a good car ride? It has been a marvelous journey with you!

How can people purchase a fine art print of these dogs?
All images in the book, as well as the outtakes, will be available as fine art prints in various sizes. Contact me for details: susanfisherphoto@gmail.com / www.susanfisherphoto.com.

Index

A

Abandoned Pet Rescue 118
Ace 16, 276
Ace bandages 81, 243
Acupuncture 3, 63, 77, 120, 195
Addison's Disease 33
Adoption
    Tips for (see shelter tips) 78
    Adopted dogs 51, 61, 81, 83, 98–99, 118–120
Adjuvant 197, 232
Aggression 154–158, 207–208, 242
Alfie 52–53
Allergies 63, 107, 167, 183–185, 190, 197, 204,
    213–217, 256, 271
American Animal Hospital Association, The 197
Angie Girl 72–73, 239
Animal chiropractor 203
Animal communication tips 258
Animal communicator 29, 239, 251
Annabel 131
Anxiety 63, 117, 133, 147, 152, 158, 210, 220,
    241–245, 252, 265
Aries 5–7, 276
Arthritis 197, 215
Atticus 8–9, 276

B

Bacall, Lauren (Cally) 96–97
Baci 122–123, 178, 275
Bach Flower Remedies 117, 220, 241, 244–245
Bahamas 200
Barlak, Michelle 38–39
Beagle xviii, 11, 47, 61
Behavioral psychology 149
Behavior analysis 149
Benko, Laura ii–iv, xii, 268–272
Benko-Rodriguez, Lisa 269
Bereavement 261–267
Betsy 140–141
Bichon 141
Birdie 116–117

Birdy 1, 105
Black Labrador 73, 127
Blindness 36–39
Bogie 96–97
Bones 180, 185 – 186
Boredom 210, 155
Boscoe 105, 240
Bowie 144–145
Boxer 31, 143
Brehm, Stephen 68
Buddy 60–61, 177, 240
Bug repellent 198
Burns 220–221
Buster 20–21, 148, 178, 239, 276

C

Cally 96–97
Calypso 126–127
Cancer 148, 189, 197–198, 200, 201, 227–237
Canine
    Canine behaviorist 59, 147, 149–157
    Canine Cognition Center 165
    Canine massage therapist 192–194
    Canine nutritionist 177, 180–187
    Canine walker 207–210
Car travel tips 139
Casey 32–33
Cavalier Spaniel 104
Cavapoo 101, 104, 131
Chaka 84–85, 239, 276
Chanel 1, 68–69, 275
Charlie (Cockapoo) 42 –43, 147
Charlie (Schnauzer / Terrier mix) 80–81
Chester 28–29, 239, 275
Chief 100–101
Chihuahua 10, 62–63, 254
Chinese Crested Mix 62–63
Chiquita 46–47
Chiropractic care 178, 203–206
Chiropractor 203–206
Chocolate Labradoodle 102–103

Chocolate Labrador 17, 120
Classical conditioning 150–151, 159
Clay 106–107, 178, 238, 277
Cockapoo 3, 42, 113–114
Codega 22–23, 275
Cody 104
Cold laser treatments 211, 215, 218
Collie 12
Conduct specialist 207
Cookie Nutella 17, 275
Cooper (English Setter) 1, 65
Cooper (Labrador Mix) 45, 178, 276
Corgi 95
Cryosurgery 195
Cystitis 223, 224

D
Daisy 48, 240, 275
Daniel 118–121
Daphne 130
Davey 1, 82–83, 275
Dawkey 30–31, 275
Deafness 9, 65, 83
Death 240, 261–267
Dental 186, 215–216, 224
Dexter 1, 102–103, 276
Diabetes 141, 215
Diarrhea 211, 220, 221, 222–223, 233
Diego 10–11
Dog
    Dog bedding 204
    Dog communicator 251–260
    Dog day care 158–164, 217
    Dog, firehouse 56
    Dog food 180–187
    Dog games 12–13, 59
    Dog health (see Body section) 176–237
    Dog interactive puzzles 170–175
    Dog psychic 247–250, 251–260
    Dog, seeing eye 36–39
    Dog trainer 153–157, 158–164
    Dog travel tips 139
    Dog walker 178, 207–210
Dora 24–25, 178
Duke 56–57, 239, 276
Dylan 74

E
Ellie 87, 240
Emergency conditions 213, 218–225
English Bulldog 69
English Cocker Spaniel 74
English Setter 65
English Springer Spaniel 133, 158
Enzo 26–27, 276
Epilepsy 21, 63
Essential oils 67, 77, 198
Exercise 152, 177–179, 204, 209–210, 251–252

F
Facts about dogs 9
Firehouse 56–57
Fish oil 201, 230
Fleas 198
Fonseca, Caio 3
Freeman, Kim 99, 178, 192–194
French Bulldog 91, 104, 115

G
Garfinkel, Eileen 239, 251–260
German Shorthaired Pointer 15
Ginger 108, 276
Glen of Imal Terrier 105
Goldendoodle 19, 33, 89, 111, 138
Golden Retriever
    English Cream Golden Retriever 21, 36, 77
    Golden 129, 164
    Light Golden Retriever 70
Gordon, David 140
Gracie 87
Great Dane 23
Greyhound
    Greyhound Friends of New Jersey 41
    Greyhound racing 119–120
    Greyhound rescue organization, Holly Dogs 119
Grief counseling 261–267
Grossman, Annie 147, 158–164

H
Harley (Cavapoo) 104
Harley (Golden Retriever) 128–129
Hauser, Sarah 117, 241, 277
Havanese 9, 135, 218

Heartworm 198–200
Hide and Seek 59
Hip dysplasia 203–204, 215
Holistic
    Holistic nutrition 177, 180–187
    Holistic pet care 177, 188–191
    Holistic veterinarian 178, 211, 256
Holistic Home Company, The xvi, 67, 198, 268, 271
Holly Dogs Greyhound Adoption 119
Homeopathy 180, 195, 213–226
Honey 34–35, 239, 251, 276
Humane Society 122, 137
Humphrey Bogart 97
HUNDE 180–187
Hydrotherapy 3, 178

I
IDEXX 202
Inhalation, gas or other material 225
Integrative medicine 195–202
iPad (training with) 148, 161
Irish Terrier xv
Isabel 10–11
Ivan 10–11
Izzy 4, 240

J
Jem 71, 275
Jenny 132–133
Jock 2–3, 178, 275

K
Kearney, Clare 177, 180–187
Kerry Blue Terrier 105
Kevin 1, 52–53
Kibble 177, 182–183, 200–201
King Charles Cavalier 48
Klein, Randy 188
Kutsch, Ginger 39

L
Labradoodle 33, 145
Labradoodle, Chocolate 103
Layla 104
Leestemaker, Luc 42

Longhaired Dachshund 25
Lou Lou 90–91, 178, 277
Lucy 1, 136–137
Lyla 10–11

M
Maddy 158
Magna Wave 201
MacLean, Evan 147, 165–169
Maltipoo
    Bacall, Lauren (Cally) 96–97
    Max 54–55
Mangold, Robert 9
Mantequilla 46–47
Massage 3, 45, 99, 178, 192–194, 262, 265, 271
Max 54–55, 239
Maxine 115, 239, 277
Maxwell, Megan E., Dr. 147, 59, 149–157
Mehmet, Oz, Dr. 202
Milk thistle 201
Miniature Goldendoodle 19, 111
Mixed Breed
    Basenji Mix 50–51
    Beagle / Hound Mix 11
    Beagle Mix 61
    Black Lab / Blue Tick Coon Hound Mix 118
    Border Collie Mix 4
    Boxer / Pit Bull Mix 57
    Bulldog / Pit Bull Mix 83
    Chihuahua / Pomeranian Mix 53
    Chinese Crested Mix 63
    Chocolate Labrador / Hound Mix 108
    Collie / German Shepherd Mix 127
    Labrador Mix 45
    Labrador / Pit Bull Mix 83
    Old English Sheepdog / Poodle Mix 117
    Poodle / Sheltie Mix 75
    Schnauzer / Terrier Mix 81
    Sharpei / Pit Bull Mix 83
    Shepherd / Hound / Dachshund Mix 137
    Shih Tzu / Bichon Mix 53
    Shih Tzu Mix 59
    Siberian Husky / German Shepard Mix 98
    Spaniel / Irish Setter / Golden Retriever Mix 78
    Spaniel Mix 78, 122

Vizsla / German Shepherd Mix 127
Yorkshire Terrier / Maltese Mix 117
Molly 1, 82–83
Monty (Goldendoodle) 88–89, 147, 177, 275–276
Monty (Soft-Coated Wheaten Terrier) 26–27
Moose 1, 108, 276
Morkie 125
Mosquito 199–200
Mulligan 1, 142–143, 276
Muppet 58–59, 147, 276

N
Nature of Animal Healing, The 195, 197
Norma Jean 82–83
Nova Scotia Duck Tolling Retriever 92
Nutrition xi, 177, 180–187, 227–232

O
Ollie (Cockapoo) 112–113
Ollie (Nova Scotia Duck Trolling Retriever) 92–93
Oncology 227, 234–237
Operant conditioning 150–151, 159
Ottosson, Nina 13, 147, 162, 170–175

P
Papillon 29
Pavlov, Ivan 150
Penny (Miniature Goldendoodle) 18–19
Penny (Nova Scotia Duck Trolling Retriever) 92
Pepper 12, 147
Pesto 1, 122, 178, 275
Plotner, Susan Fisher xi, xvii, 272, 274
Poppy 62–63, 275
Prebiotics 201
Probiotics 67, 77, 201, 215
Prozac 256
Psychic medium 239, 247
Pug 16
Puggle 47
Pulsed Electro Magnetic Frequency 201
Puppy
    Bowie 144–145
    Thor 94–95

Q
Quassia bark powder 119

R
Rainbow bridge 249
Rashes 221
Raw diet 182, 184–185, 200
Reiki 117, 195, 239, 241–242, 277
Rex 32–33, 275
Rhodesian Ridgeback 47
Rhodie 110–111, 147–148, 239, 275
Richard, Paul 76
Riley 93
Rookie 124–125, 240
Rosie (Beagle) xvii–xix, 170
Rosie (Black Labrador) 73
Ruby 1, 82–83, 275
Rugby 78–79, 275
Russian Toy 35
Russo, Kim 239, 247–250

S
Schnoodle 97
School for The Dogs 77, 147, 158–165
Sedona 98, 178, 276
Seeing Eye dog 36
Seeing Eye®, The 36, 38–39, 270, 277
Senisi, Kate 158, 163
Shane 14–15, 276
Shelter tips 78
Shep 126–127
Show dog 15, 63
Siberian Huskie 98
Silky Yorkshire Terrier 73
Simba 36–39, 148, 269, 277
Smith Ridge Veterinary Center 195
Smokey 75
Smokey (Dr. Gerald Post) 235–237
Soft-Coated Wheaten Terrier 27
Sonya 50–51, 276
Standard Poodle 130
Stella 62–63, 275
Sunny 66–67, 178, 276

T
Tate 76–77, 178, 270
Teva 126–127
Thor 94–95, 276
Three–legged dog 45, 178, 276
ThunderShirt™ 117
Ticks 198
Toby 134–135, 240
Toro Jones 82–83
Toxic
    Foods to avoid 129
    Treatment for poisoning 221
Trauma 218–220, 234, 242
Truman 62–63
Tug 132–133
Turbo 1, 136–137
Turley, Laura 178, 207

U
Unknown Breed 137, 67, 122

V
Vaccination 179, 197–198, 200, 216, 232, 270
Van de Poll, Wendy 49, 240, 261
Venus 62–63, 275
Veterinarian
    Dr. Jill Elliot 178, 211
    Dr. Gene Giggleman 178, 203
    Dr. Marty Goldstein 178, 195, 277
    Dr. Gerald Post 178, 227
Veterinary Cancer Center, The 178, 227

Vomiting 220–233

W
Wally 116–117
Water
Bottle 160
Bowl 122
Playing with 114
Swimming 122
Therapies with 213–214, 217, 219–220, 245
Welsh Springer Spaniel 93
West Highland Terrier 71
Wheaten Terrier 27
Whiskers Holistic Pet Care 77, 177, 188
Winnie 20, 114, 275
Wounds 220, 221
Wrigley 70

X
Xoloitzcuintli 63
Xylitol 129

Y
Yellow Labrador 108
Yogi xiv–xv, 270
Yorkshire Terrier 73, 85, 117

Z
Zero 40–41, 276
Zoey 118, 240
Zuzu 138–139